Get Hired . . . It's Your Job

Also by Stephen C. Rafe

How to Be Prepared to Think on Your Feet
(Harper Business, 1990)

Get Hired
It's Your Job

Stephen C. Rafe

HarperBusiness
A Division of HarperCollins*Publishers*

International Standard Book Number: 0-88730-438-9

Library of Congress Catalog Card Number: 90–47896

Library of Congress Cataloging-in-Publication Data

Rafe, Stephen C.
    Get hired— it's your job / Stephen C. Rafe.
      p.   cm.
    Includes bibliographical references and index.
    1. Job hunting.   2. Employment interviewing.   I. Title.
    HF5382.7.R34   1990
    640.14—dc20   90–47896
                                                     CIP

PRINTED IN THE UNITED STATES OF AMERICA

90 91 92 93 CC/HC 9 8 7 6 5 4 3 2 1

To the loyal friends and loved ones who provide boundless faith and confidence to the fine executives who need them as they face joblessness and go on to win. Your caring does *make the difference. I know.*

Contents

Introduction ix

Part One: Steps Leading to Job Interviews

1 Where You've Been, Where You're Headed 3
2 Organizing Your Material 14
3 Career Moves 27
4 Packaging the "Product" 34
5 Approaching the Market 58
6 Building Your Job Leads 67

Part Two: The Employment Interview

7 Preparing for Interviews 87
8 The Three Parts of an Interview 104
9 Upon Arrival 111
10 The Interview Environment 116
11 The Interviewer's Attitude 119
12 Establishing Rapport 126
13 The Four Types of Interviews 133

14 What You Will Be Asked   137

15 It's Your Turn   148

16 Dealing with Questioners and
    Disagreements   155

17 How to Avoid Misunderstandings   162

18 Special Considerations   167

19 Closing the Meeting   176

20 Your Reactions   180

Part Three: The Follow-up

21 How to Follow Up   189

22 Callbacks   196

23 Once You're Hired   202

    Epilogue   209

    Reading List   211

    Index   215

Introduction

In the job marketplace, you may be competing against five, fifty, or even a hundred seemingly qualified applicants for a single managerial, technical, or professional job. Leading daily newspapers report 200 to 500 responses to a single classified ad even when the employer is not identified. Personnel agencies have résumés pouring in by the thousands. Headhunters turn away more people than they recruit.

If you are about to enter the job market or expect to make a career move someday, you need a strong, positive approach. The program outlined here provides you with the plan you need; it has been tested and proven successful for people in all fields.

This book had its beginnings in the *E*mployment *S*earch *P*rogram™ seminars I conducted at the New School for Social Research in New York City several years ago. It has been offered through the New Skills Bank Program of the National Urban League, to women's groups, to the chronically unemployed, to graduating students from nearly fifty colleges and universities at national seminars, and to private clients up through the CEO level. Now you will have the benefit of every refinement that has been made in the program; you will gain from techniques that have helped even the chronically unemployed make successful career connections. This book will help anyone who is considering changing employers, who is presently unemployed, or who wants to understand the employment search process better.

A number of books have been written on how to find a job, but most of them concentrate on how to write a résumé and conduct a search. That is not where help is needed most. After all, what good are a great résumé and a thorough search if you can't survive the interview? In these pages you will learn how to develop all the tools and information you need to find a job. Most important of all, you will learn how to understand and evaluate every aspect of an interview—even under the pressure of dealing with the unfamiliar.

In the *E*mployment *S*earch *P*rogram™ I designed and conducted, in the seminars, and in private consultations with "de-hired" executives, the questions have centered on one area: the interview itself. This book is written about that area: how to prepare for an interview, how to ensure a successful one, and how to follow it up. Although you may be tempted to skip right to the interview section, you will best serve your needs by reading the book straight through before settling down with any part of it.

Sometimes you will be encouraged to make copies of forms that will help you with your record keeping and other aspects of your employment search. You will learn how to assess your background and qualifications for the position you have in mind; you will learn how to develop the tools you need to conduct a successful search; and you will discover how to select the employer that suits *you* best. As you progress through it, you will find that the book shows you how to use proven marketing techniques to conduct your search as though you were selling the most valuable commodity in the world—and you are.

If you are in the job market or are considering a move, you will indeed be competing in a marketplace—one in which the buyer is trying to go beyond your skills and services to determine how you might fit in better than your competitors. You are presumed to be qualified, or you would not be having an interview at all. What matters, then, is how you handle your interpersonal contacts with the employer. This book will show you how to evaluate yourself as your product, zero in on the best market for it, develop a sound approach to the market, and then make the sale.

Part One
Steps Leading to Job Interviews

1
Where You've Been, Where You're Headed

Knowing where you've been in your career is prerequisite to knowing where you're headed—perhaps for the rest of your professional life. If you have just been "de-hired," the chances are good that your employer's action has little to do with either you or your potential worth to another employer.

Organizations preach loyalty, and at one time in our history there were many opportunities to spend entire careers in one place. Now, however, mergers, acquisitions, downsizings, bankruptcies, and worse have shown us that loyalty can often be a one-way street.

Although this book does not view careers as a form of king of the hill or jungle combat, you need to remember that unswerving loyalty—although expected and even demanded—may one day be rewarded with a golden parachute, a golden handshake, or just a face-saving comment or two as the door closes on your way out.

In the managerial and executive ranks, what goes around does indeed come around, more frequently than we might think. The department head who interviews you may have come to that position after being let go somewhere else. Given enough time, you may find some of the people who aided or abetted in your de-hiring out on the streets themselves. More than a few executives have shared that experience with me, and I once had a supervisor who gave me the bad news hint that he himself was in need of a job and that I might be able to help him.

The motto? The Boy Scouts of America have it right: Be prepared! Then if you suddenly find the door closing behind you—for whatever reason—you will be ready to continue your career elsewhere with little interruption. That door often closes because, during critical times, only

3

the strong survive. The question is: strong in terms of what? That's one of the many areas we'll explore. But first we need to consider who you are and where you want to be.

What Have You Done?

Most prospective employers will want to know how you answer the question "What have you done?" As you will see later in the book, there are many ways in which you might respond, and your answer will depend upon the skills you acquire for determining the interviewer's needs. Regardless of the response you choose, however, you will have to be prepared to back it up with specific, concrete information.

Where Are You Most Successful?

Like several other areas a prospective employer will have to explore, the question "Where are you most successful?" can lend itself to many responses. Again the key is to learn where the interviewer wants you to go and be prepared to follow that lead.

The first step is knowing your strengths, the attributes that make you unique. The accompanying list will help you consider some of the many positive points that could realistically be made about you.

What Do You Like?

"What do you like?" also might appear to be a disarmingly simple question, but in fact, a considerable amount of forethought is prerequisite to having the right answer at hand when something like this is asked. Certainly, it would be to your advantage to show that you have already given the matter some thought.

Regrettably, there is no handy chart for this one, and it is doubtful that one could be developed. We can, however, provide you with some thought-starters that will lead you in the right direction.

Think back to a job that you have held—any job. Put yourself in an environment that you experienced within that job. Now go to a situation that will make you feel warm all over—not just attitudinally, but also physically warm as you think about it. Jot down the experience, and look

IDENTIFY YOUR STRENGTHS

The personal strengths listed below can make a critical difference in the selection of a candidate for employment at various levels and in various careers. Make a copy of the list and circle each word that applies to you, or, on a separate piece of paper, write down *all* the words that describe you as you are now. Then look back over the list and place check marks next to the words that describe you *most.*

When you read further in this book and begin to consider the personality traits required for different careers and management levels, your list of strengths will help you make certain decisions more appropriately than you otherwise might.

Academic	Creative	Idealistic	Peaceable	Spontaneous
Active	Curious	Imaginative	Perceptive	Spirited
Accurate	Daring	Independent	Persevering	Stable
Adaptable	Deliberate	Individualistic	Pleasant	Steady
Adventurous	Democratic	Industrious	Poised	Strong
Affectionate	Dependable	Informal	Polite	Strong-minded
Aggressive	Determined	Ingenious	Practical	Sympathetic
Alert	Dignified	Intellectual	Precise	Tactful
Ambitious	Discreet	Intelligent	Progressive	Teachable
Artistic	Dominant	Inventive	Prudent	Tenacious
Assertive	Eager	Kind	Purposeful	Thorough
Attractive	Easygoing	Leisurely	Quick	Thoughtful
Bold	Efficient	Lighthearted	Quiet	Tolerant
Broadminded	Emotional	Likable	Rational	Tough
Businesslike	Energetic	Logical	Realistic	Trusting
Calm	Enterprising	Loyal	Reasonable	Trustworthy
Capable	Enthusiastic	Mature	Reflective	Unaffected
Careful	Fair-minded	Methodical	Relaxed	Unassuming
Cautious	Farsighted	Meticulous	Reliable	Understanding
Charming	Firm	Mild	Reserved	Unexcitable
Cheerful	Flexible	Moderate	Resourceful	Uninhibited
Clear-thinking	Forceful	Modest	Responsible	Verbal
Clever	Formal	Natural	Retiring	Versatile
Competent	Frank	Obliging	Robust	Warm
Competitive	Friendly	Open-minded	Self-confident	Wholesome
Confident	Generous	Opportunistic	Self-controlled	Wise
Conscientious	Gentle	Optimistic	Sensible	Witty
Conservative	Good-natured	Organized	Sensitive	Zany
Considerate	Healthy	Original	Serious	
Cool	Helpful	Outgoing	Sharp-witted	
Cooperative	Honest	Painstaking	Sincere	
Courageous	Humorous	Patient	Sociable	

Be sure to add any additional words you believe describe you.

at what you have written. Did the satisfaction come from something only you knew you did? Or did it come from something someone said?

Internal. If the source of satisfaction came from within, was it because you either proved something or showed somebody it could be done? Because of what it did for someone else? Because it brought you closer to others? Because you felt in control or took charge successfully?

External. If the satisfaction came from others' responses, did it come from recognition of your leadership skills? Your achievements? Your ability to get along with others or work within a team?

Basically, your responses to these questions will help you determine (1) whether you depend on internal or external sources for feeling good about your life and (2) whether you derive the greatest satisfaction from activities based on power, affiliation, or achievement.

It is important to know what motivates you before you even schedule a job interview. Suppose, for example, that you tend to be heavily power-oriented and that you have a strong need to receive recognition from others to gain personal satisfaction. In that case, you may want to steer clear of an organization in which your power drives would be thwarted by a superior who gives you no feedback.

Internal People. Generally, people who get their satisfaction from within are internally oriented. Often they are independent thinkers who need little reinforcement from others as motivation. To go further, they may also tend to do well when they work independently of others. For that reason, they may be more oriented toward achievement than toward power or affiliation.

External People. On the other hand, people who rely on others as a source of satisfaction may be mostly oriented toward power or affiliation. If power is their main drive, they often do best when they can lead projects. If affiliation is a stronger drive, they may function at their peak when they are part of a team effort.

Of course, it is possible that you have some of each drive within you; you may sometimes gain from self-satisfaction and at other times be most reinforced by the compliments of others. What you should look for here is a pattern, a way to help yourself predict the circumstances that will be most to your liking.

What Would You Like to Do?

When an interviewer asks you what you would like to do, you might find yourself giving an entirely different answer from that which was expected or wanted. The key, again, is to prepare yourself. The insights you gain here will help, and later you will learn how to elicit the interviewer's intent before you respond to such questions. At this time, however, you should consider your options. You want to have a variety of responses at hand when you go into the interview.

MOTIVATORS
In asking the question, the interviewer may want to know what motivates you. Using the information we just covered, you can see that the interviewer may have an overbalance of power, achievement, or affiliation as a personal drive. Therefore, the interviewer's views of you will reflect the drive you convey in your response. He or she may also have some specific views on what the criteria for the job entail in terms of power, achievement, and affiliation.

YOUR BEST BET
To be on the safe side, you will first need to know which drive will be the safest one to communicate, and you will then have to develop a reply that best displays it. Don't wait until the middle of a crucial interview to begin to consider either your response or your strategy.

Take the time to review all the data you develop as you read this book. Then prepare separate statements that will demonstrate something that you like to *do* in terms of power, achievement, and affiliation. That will help you to be prepared and at your best even when you must be alert and attentive to all the other aspects of the interview.

Are Your Expectations Realistic?

Another categorical question that the interviewer may have in mind is whether your expectations are realistic. In this case, however, the question may never be voiced. Instead, the interviewer may seek the information through inferences based on your responses to other questions.

Joseph P. Yeager developed what is called the Yeager Performance Model, and he has given permission to adapt this information to help you succeed in the employment interview.

WHAT THIS MEANS TO YOU
The people who interview you will assess your past and present performance in light of the requirements of the position you are seeking.

THE YEAGER PERFORMANCE MODEL

An individual's level of present or past performance can be divided into three major categories. Does he or she *want to, know how to,* and *have the chance to* achieve the objectives at issue?

The assessment can be made by asking key questions in each area, and the responses can provide the basis for a reasonably accurate prediction of how well the individual is likely to perform. The questions deal with motivation, means, and opportunity to succeed.

Did the Candidate Want to:

- Do what is required?
- Work for the kinds of incentives and payoffs that the job offers?
- Demonstrate the appropriate level of independence and power for this job?
- Supervise at the appropriate level for this job?
- Achieve the same outcomes and goals as the boss?
- Engage in social contact at a level appropriate for this job?
- Hide something that would embarrass him or her?
- Get along with others as required or necessary?
- Be competitive and assertive as needed versus dependent and passive?
- Stay in the job for the wrong reasons (e.g., status versus job interest)?
- Resolve conflicts about the job? For example, in an aggressive job, will the individual's beliefs and self-image place him or her in conflict with the job?

Did the Candidate Know How To:

- Perform the procedures, processes, and techniques to do the job?
- Use the right strategy for solving the problems that occur on the job?
- Use the right political or persuasive skills to get cooperation?
- Use interpersonal and technical skills?
- Elicit cooperation, motivation, and coordination? Sell ideas?
- Sound as though he or she is camouflaging a weak know-how?
- Carry out the job's technical aspects? Are his or her skills current?

Did the Candidate Have the Chance to Carry Out the Responsibility Appropriately and Effectively? Did He or She Have:

- The authority to match the responsibility?
- The right kind of position or title to elicit cooperation?

- The information, tools, and working conditions he or she needs for success?
- The right incentives and payoffs to make him or her want to work?
- The right kind of supervision to elicit his or her skills, rapport, and cooperation?
- Deadlines or demands of equal priority that place his or her skills in conflict?
- The financial, human, or technical resources to do the job?
- Accurate feedback on his or her performance essential to adapting as needed?

Look over my adaptation of the Yeager Performance Model again and ask yourself how it might apply whenever you have the need to discuss a less than desirable aspect of your career either present or past.

For example, if you had difficulty in carrying out some task, was it because the task was something you didn't want to do (and may not have to do in a future job); because you didn't know how to do it (and may not have had the proper training for it); or because you lacked the chance to do it (for any number of reasons already covered)?

If you lacked the motivation, means, or opportunity to be successful, you may have to explain that in terms the interviewer can understand and accept. You will be on the most solid ground if you would not be expected to perform that particular task on the new job or if it would not constitute a major portion of your duties.

APPLYING THE MODEL

Thurmond was fired from his last position. He had been highly motivated, and he knew how to perform the procedures, processes, and techniques for getting the job done. However, he was in the middle of a political hotbed not of his own making, and he was an achievement-oriented person and a self-starter with less emphasis on power and affiliation modes. He knew how to establish schedules and deadlines, and he attempted to delegate appropriately. He was flexible enough to adapt to the projects he was given and to the people assigned to him for those projects.

However, some of the people he needed to rely on did not report directly to him. One or two who knew that used their other supervisor's work as an excuse for putting off Thurmond's assignments. His own boss, to whom both he and the other supervisor reported, did not take charge of the situation, and that made Thurmond appear to be the bad guy. His boss gave him little direction when it came to establishing deadlines or priorities for projects. Sometimes, his boss would abandon him when others—particularly higher-ups—criticized a lack of productivity from his group.

Lacking essential support, Thurmond was ultimately fired. Regardless of the reason, fact is fact, and during his interviews, it was up to Thurmond to be prepared to present his case in a way that would evoke understanding (but not sympathy) from interviewers. He could neither bad-mouth others nor seek pity for himself. He had to be straightforward, matter-of-fact, and as unemotional as possible. Anger toward the former organization or his boss would not get him anywhere, and neither would complaining. Yet prior to my work with him, Thurmond had both expressed anger and complained during interviews before he realized that it was up to him to assess each of the negative situations in his career and explain it briefly in terms that the Yeager model provides.

Knowing Yourself Even Better

Before you start accepting interviews, it helps to know even more about yourself. Many personality tests are available to those who want to use them as tools for self-assessment. (Later, we'll talk a bit about employers' uses of these tests.) Some tests, such as the Myers-Briggs, enable you to examine who you are in considerable depth and come up with a detailed profile. Most psychologists in the Yellow Pages can either set up such testing for you or refer you to someone who provides the service. So can some career-counseling firms. However, both testing and counseling can be costly, and you might not want to invest the time and money at this stage.

Yet you might benefit from having a bit more insight into your personality. The LaHaye Temperament Analysis, referred to in the Reading List at the end of this book, provides such a test, along with a detailed analysis that offers concrete guidance.

LaHaye's test is based on a model that goes all the way back to Solomon, over 1000 years before Christ, was modified by Hippocrates, and was expanded upon by a physician named Galen early in the third century. The test delineates four temperaments—sanguine, choleric, melancholic, and phlegmatic—and presents twelve possible combinations by establishing one of the types as dominant and a second type as subordinate. The types are relatively easy to understand.

Sanguines and cholerics tend to be externally oriented; they face

outward and display more concern for others. Melancholics and phleg-
matics tend to be internally oriented; they face inward and show more
concern for themselves.

THE RAFE MODEL

To help busy executives understand themselves and others quickly and
make off-the-cuff guesses that lead to better communication, I adapted
the four-temperament theory to the polarities of approach and avoidance
behavior. I label the temperaments Approach I, Approach II, Avoidance
I, and Avoidance II.

No one can say which type is best because it would first be necessary to establish the meaning of "best." If wealth were meant, for
example, it might be useful to know that some of the world's wealthiest
people fall into the Avoidance I and II categories.

During most executive-level interviews, candidates are well advised
to display a balanced mix of Approach I and Approach II traits. They will
then come across as enthusiastic and outgoing (Approach I) and yet
relaxed and receptive (Approach II).

However, this is a generalization that may not apply to some careers. In addition, the interviewer's personality may dictate, at least in
part, which mode would be most likely to succeed at that moment.

If you feel that you are an Approach-oriented person, ask yourself
whether you approach others (Approach I) or are receptive to their
approaches (Approach II). If you believe you are Avoidance-oriented,
ask yourself whether you try to keep others away from you (Avoidance
I) or tend to withdraw from others (Avoidance II).

Approach I (Active–Gregarious) Words, voice tones, and body language combine to say, "I want to approach you."

Approach II (Passive–Reticent but Friendly) Words, voice tones, and
body language combine to say, "I would accept an approach from you
to me."

Avoidance I (Active–Hostile, Aggressive) Words, voice tones, and
body language combine to say, "I want to keep you away from me."

Avoidance II (Passive–Fearful, Insecure) Words, voice tones, and
body language combine to say, "I want to keep me away from you."

To explore these preliminary assessments further, consider the
information that follows to see which one might describe you—particularly during an employment interview.

Approach Modes. To determine whether you are an Approach person, ask yourself these kinds of questions:

Do you tend to come on strong? Do you often take over or monopolize conversations? Do you seek attention? Do you tend to overdo your praises of others? Do others find it difficult to get a word in edgewise? Do you spend considerable time trying to push your own ideas and points even when others can offer valid counterpoints?

Do you tend to be brutally frank and tell it like it is? Do you sometimes reveal more than you should? Do you sometimes resort to sweeping generalities and leave out key details along the way?

Do you tend to downplay situations or try to sweep things under the rug?

Do you sometimes start to express your views and then back off? Do you yield to others, perhaps more readily than you should? Are you generally supportive of others? Do you feel relaxed and appropriately assertive when you communicate?

Are your overall messages (words, voice tones, nonverbals) active or passive?

Avoidance Modes. If you feel that you are Avoidance-oriented, these questions may help you check this out further:

Do you sometimes (frequently, always) feel offended? Ignored? Treated poorly? Put off? Given the runaround?

Specifically, do you need to impress, to persuade, or to be treated according to your set expectations?

Do you tend to attack or criticize others? Do you engage in faultfinding or blame laying? Do you sometimes put people down? Do you make demands of others? Do you set expectations for others in your relationships that they find difficult to fulfill? Are your expectations implied, or do you state them clearly?

Do you feel the need to be in control?

Your voice tones and nonverbal signals can tell you more about yourself than your words alone can say. Consider whether the signals you transmit tend to encourage people to unite with you or to keep their distance.

- An Approach I is likely to appear relaxed and lean forward with open posture.
- An Approach II is likely to appear relaxed and sit upright with open posture.
- An Avoidance I is likely to appear tense and lean to one side with closed posture.
- An Avoidance II is likely to appear tense and lean back with closed posture.

Monitor your messages and ask yourself what conveys these impressions. Ask close friends and family members to give you *constructive* feedback in these areas. Ask them to describe your actions or give you their views on what seems to motivate them. Ask them also whether your total communication (words, tones, nonverbals) sends clear messages or confuses others. Try to find out what accounts for that. Explore the intensity of the messages. Do you overdo or underdo the signals?

Remember not to judge either yourself or the feedback your critics give you. Your purpose should be to *understand yourself better* so you can make the appropriate adjustments to each situation.

Once again, everyone has varying elements of the four types in his or her personality, and one type may merely predominate during your interviews. This, then, is the primary purpose for providing an assessment tool here: To help you understand yourself better so you can use the insight to have the best possible outcomes from the meetings.

Later in this book, you will learn how to apply this technique to others even during your interviews, so practice it on yourself now. Get comfortable with it. Then you will come to know yourself and others better, and that will lead to better communication by everyone.

2
Organizing Your Material

Once you have a better understanding of who you are, where you've been, and where you're headed, you can develop more specific tools. You will need them for a search that will lead to more and better interviews. To help yourself develop those tools more effectively, you must do a little brainstorming. The best approach is to have a tape recorder running during this exercise, because you can speak faster than you can write. Ask yourself the first question aloud, answer it aloud, and then go on to the next question. When you have answered all the questions, start at the first question again and proceed through the list once more. Do this until you have exhausted your ability to respond to the questions.

Skills and Experience Inventory

With this much information in place, your next step is to begin to put the data together for easy access when you need to prepare a résumé or rehearse for an interview. Here you will record more specific, career-based information about yourself. Either make copies of the pages provided and complete the copies, or record the data elsewhere. In any case, be sure to get everything down on paper before you try to go any further. Doing so will save you a considerable amount of time now and will help you have more accurate input later.

EVALUATION OF PAST EXPERIENCES

The following experience: (List things that stand out most in your memory.)	*Helped me to become better at:* (List skills, abilities, and personality traits that prove you became a better employee as a result of each experience.)

At home

_____

_____ _____

In elementary and high school

_____

_____ _____

In college

_____

_____ _____

In military service

_____

_____ _____

In the community

_____

_____ _____

In memberships

_____

_____ _____

In hobbies and interests

_____

_____ _____

In work experiences

_____

_____ _____

In relationships with others

_____   _____

_____   _____

Write down the *most important* abilities you have acquired (from among those listed here)

_____   _____

_____   _____

_____   _____

SKILLS INVENTORY
(Make copies of this entire checklist and complete each entry.)

Personal Data

- Name

- Address

- Phone number

- Social Security number

- Academic background

- Professional affiliations

(Now complete a separate sheet for the following. Provide the information regardless of how relevant you think it might be to an employment search.)

Education

- Schools attended

- Dates

- Degrees earned

- Other career training

- Best subjects

- Grades

- Subjects enjoyed most

- Academic achievements

- Memberships and activities

Off-the-Job Activities

- Related to your skills and achievements

- Related to your leadership and management abilities

- Related to your ability to work with others

- Volunteer and not-for-profit organizations in which you have carried out the above

Aptitudes
(Describe your skills in each of the following areas.)

- Verbal

- Mathematics and science

- Problem solving

- Supervisory, administrative, organizational

EMPLOYMENT RECORD
(Make as many copies of this checklist as you need, and complete one copy
for each employer.)

Employer

- Name

- Highest position held

- Dates

Experience

- All jobs held

- Locations and dates

- Types of employers

- Employers' lines of business

Supervisory Experience

- Number of people supervised

- Their positions or functions

- Examples of your leadership skills

Functional Skills

- Skills acquired

- Functions performed

- Special accomplishments

- Areas of efficiency and effectiveness

Special Interests
(Areas of personal, job-related interest)

Evaluation of Past Experiences

Throughout your interviews, you may frequently be asked to demonstrate how your experiences have helped you grow in some way. As with some of the other areas we have discussed, it can sometimes be tough to come up with this information under the stress of an employment interview. Why subject yourself to additional tension? Prepare now; rehearse later; and you will be that much further ahead when such questions come up during an interview.

Preparing a Personal Balance Sheet

Now that you have recorded your many good points, it is time to put some things in perspective. No one is skilled at everything. In fact, you may privately rank your skills in some aspects of your own career below a five on a scale of one to ten.

Here is your opportunity to assess your least strong points and record them in one place. Doing so will give you better perspective for conducting your search, because knowing what you're *not* good at can be just as important to finding the right job as knowing what you do well. To make dealing with the bad news easier, use the format that follows to balance each weakness against your strong points.

Personal Assessment

As you continue to develop this realistic appraisal of yourself, you will undoubtedly think about your past employment in terms of the people with whom you worked. This is your opportunity to consider that aspect of your career in greater depth.

Think about your relationships with others and your interactions with them. Consider where you have been most and least successful. Reflect on the situations themselves. Then go through the yes and no questions that follow and check off the responses that seem most consistently applicable to your career to date. There are no right answers; there is no magic formula at the end to tell you where you should be. Instead, this checklist should provide an additional way for you to consider that question yourself.

EVALUATION OF PAST EXPERIENCES

The following experiences
(List the things that stand out most in your memory.)

- At home

- In elementary and high school

- In college

- In college and military service

- In the community

- In memberships

- In hobbies and interests

Helped me to become better at
(List skills, abilities, and personality traits that will show you to be a better employee as a result of each experience.)

- In hobbies and interests

- In work experiences

- In relationships with others

- Above all

- (List the most important abilities you have acquired, from those listed here.)

BALANCE SHEET

Your Strongest Points: *Your Least Strong Points:*
General   Personality General

_____   _____
_____   _____
_____   _____
_____   _____

Job related   Personality Job-related

_____   _____
_____   _____
_____   _____

                                 Academic

_____   _____
_____   _____

                                 Skills

_____   _____
_____   _____

                                 Related
                                 interests

_____   _____
_____   _____

                                 Career
                                 field

_____   _____
_____   _____
_____   _____

PERSONAL ASSESSMENT—WORKING WITH PEOPLE (INTERNAL/EXTERNAL)

Yes   *No*

____   ____   Do you consider yourself to be sociable and gregarious?

____   ____   Do you prefer to work surrounded by lots of other people?

____   ____   Is this the environment in which you function most effectively?

____   ____   Would you prefer to have your own work to do, without much interaction with other people?

____   ____   Would you prefer to have your own work, but with much interaction, liaison, and coordination with coworkers?

____   ____   Are you a dyed-in-the-wool teamworker who thrives on shared responsibility?

____   ____   Are you a loner who prefers to take responsibility for your own job, which will grow in size as you become more experienced?

____   ____   Do you prefer a relaxed and informal relationship with other people?

____   ____   Do you prefer fairly structured and formal situations?

____   ____   Do you like to work for one person?

____   ____   Do you enjoy working with two or more people?

____   ____   Do you like to help other people?

____   ____   Does this include people in the same office?

____   ____   Do you like to help or assist one person all the time?

____   ____   Do you like to assist lots of different people one after the other?

____   ____   Do you like to assist lots of different people simultaneously?

____   ____   Can you, or could you, delegate work to others but accept responsibility for the results?

____   ____   Do you want to supervise people (work through others) to reach specific goals?

____ ____ Do you deal best with many people at a time?

____ ____ Do you deal best with one person at a time?

____ ____ Do you prefer to work with people your own age?

____ ____ Do you prefer to work with people younger than yourself?

____ ____ Do you prefer to work with people older than yourself?

____ ____ Do you like to research or elicit information?

____ ____ Is getting results important to you?

____ ____ Is persuading or selling important to you?

____ ____ Is teaching or mentoring important to you?

____ ____ Would you like your work to deal primarily with mediating?

____ ____ Do you want to provide a service?

____ ____ Is the social or financial betterment of others important to you?

____ ____ Is the improvement of the quality of life important to you?

____ ____ Do you prefer to have little or no contact with others, but do you want the results of your work to benefit people generally?

Again, these questions are not intended to be subjected to some form of evaluation; in fact, they are not even all-inclusive. As you think about your responses to them, you may come up with several other issues that are just as important to you and to your future.

Write Your Ideal Job-Offer Advertisement

You can now begin to focus in on the criteria for jobs for which you might be best qualified or which you would find most attractive. One handy way to do this is to read several display advertisements in the employment section of a major newspaper and then use the better ones as models for ads you will write about yourself.

Since there are often discrepancies between the job you are best qualified for and the job you would most like to have, it will be important for you to write an ad for each one and then compare the differences.

The Job That Describes You Best   *Aspect*

_____   Credentials expected

_____

_____   Experience

_____

_____   Special skills
_____   Type of employer

_____

_____   Industry or field

_____

_____   Location of job

The Job You Would Like to Have Most   *Aspect*

_____   Credentials expected

_____

_____   Experience

_____

_____   Special skills

_____

_____   Type of employer

_____

_____   Industry or field

_____

_____   Location of job

_____

As you developed each ad, did you notice the differences between the real and the ideal—what you are qualified for as compared with what you might want to have? This may not be the time to reconcile the differences, particularly if you need a job now. In the best interests of your professional future, however, you will want to give serious thought to developing a plan that will prepare you for that perfect position. In the meantime, your comparison of the ads will enable you to put your skills in more realistic perspective before you begin your job search in earnest.

Write Your Retirement Speech

Once again, to help you decide where you are going with your career, we will ask you to play a game of "imagine with me." In this case, the objective will be to enable you to focus on what you want to do with the rest of your professional life. The ads you just wrote have given you a start, and this assignment will provide the rest of that picture.

Pretend that you have been asked to write the remarks that will be made at your retirement dinner. You have reached the end of your business career, and this will be your final moment in the limelight. It will be your last opportunity to let the world know what you have done with your life.

As you write these remarks, be sure to include at least the following points:

- Years spent with employer
- Positions attained
- Areas of responsibility
- Honors received
- Recognition gained
- Attitude and personality
- What you will best be remembered for

Some Serious Thought

This exercise should get you thinking about a lot of things. Regardless of your current age or health, once you begin to think seriously about your final career days, some interesting things begin to happen. Some executives who have gone through the steps prescribed so far have said that they had many conflicting thoughts when they did the retirement speech exercise. Some even changed careers after considering themselves and their business futures in that much depth. One person went back to school and became a minister; another became a college professor; several others undertook further education to make significant changes in their qualifications within their careers.

The key here is to know yourself better. As Shakespeare put it in *Hamlet:* "This above all: to thine own self be true."

3
Career Moves

According to some estimates, people in managerial, executive, and professional positions make career moves every five years or less. The moves may occur within the same field, the same organization, the same department, or the same specialty area. Most moves, however, are from one organization to another within the same or a similar field and in the same career area, and they often include changes in responsibilities. Unless the organization is downsizing or disbanding, most of the moves create new openings. This book will deal directly with the strategies for finding career positions *outside* your present organization.

Until now, you have considered who you are, where you have been, and where you would like to go. You have also given considerable thought to other aspects of yourself as an executive or a manager. This will be your opportunity to consider where you would like to invest your career. There may not be enough time for you to make significant changes in your skills for a job you want, but there is much you can do to choose the business or industry in which you would like to work, the areas within your field that are most attractive to you, the kind of organization in which you would like to be employed, and the location that appeals to you most.

Profiling Potential Employers

Use this opportunity to record the information that will tell you where you are most likely to do your best work.

THE ADVANTAGES OF LARGE AND SMALL EMPLOYERS

A Large Employer:

- Frequently offers a higher starting salary
- May have greater potential earnings
- May provide more fringe benefits
- May have more job levels for promotions
- Often has a policy of promotion from within
- Frequently has a system or plan for advancement
- May provide desirable training programs
- May offer greater security
- May be able to fall back on financial strength in hard times
- May have more money for research and development
- Could provide more staff for problem solving
- Frequently has diverse operations and transfer opportunities
- Could be less vulnerable to mergers and subsequent job dissolution

A Small Employer:

- Frequently provides faster recognition
- May not have as much internal competition
- May provide quicker advancement
- Often enables employees to assume responsibility quickly
- May provide a chance to participate actively
- Often enables executives to see the results of their own work
- May offer opportunity to participate in ownership
- Frequently provides a chance to grow as the firm grows
- May be especially attractive to self-starters
- Offers varied work
- Is less likely to relocate employees
- Can be more flexible with its business policies
- Could be good grooming for owning a business

WHAT APPEALS TO YOU?

As you consider which of these possibilities appeal to you most, also give thought to where you might realistically fit in. Keep in mind your ad-writing exercise, in which you assessed the differences between the real and the ideal when it comes to what you are best qualified for and what you desire most. This is the time to ensure that you will fit in well with the kinds of employers you have in mind.

WHERE YOU ARE LIKELY TO SUCCEED
This next exercise will give you the opportunity to home in on the kinds of employers that would suit you best. Use the chart to find where you should be looking so you can advance toward the perfect résumé and the perfect interview.

How to Assess an Organization

You have been narrowing down, becoming increasingly specific about who you are, and becoming more selective about where you want to work. This is certainly not consistent with the attitude of "I'll take any job, anywhere, at any salary" that is often voiced in panic by unemployed executives. It is an important key to maintaining your self-esteem. After all, you must feel good about who you are if you are going to sell yourself to others. The process also enables you to become more realistic about the employers among which you are most likely to find the best opportunities.

There are any number of directories that describe organizations and provide profiles, and still others that profile the executives of those organizations. One approach might be to start with a reference such as the Dun & Bradstreet *Million Dollar Directories* or Thomas' *Register of American Manufacturers.* (If your potential employer would not be listed in one of these directories, consult the *Directory of Directories.* There is a directory for almost any field you can describe.) Look up potential employers according to your field or by geographical area, depending on which is your higher priority. Once you have gained all the information you can from directories, look up key executives in *Standard & Poors;* a directory that lists executives in your specific field; and the various *Who's Who* publications.

The key directories listed at the end of this book will provide a starting point during your next trip to the library. While at the library, look through the most recently published books describing the best employers or the best places to work in the United States.

You should also check the *Reader's Guide to Periodical Literature* and/or the *Industrial Arts Index* for recent articles on the fields, types of employers, and specific organizations that interest you most.

CHOOSING YOUR EMPLOYER

I would prefer to work for the following kind of employer:

_____ Corporation

_____ Counseling firm

_____ Government agency

_____ Union

_____ Trade association

_____ Not-for-profit in _____
                         (field)

I would prefer to work for an employer of the following *size:*

_____ Small in dollars

_____ Small in personnel

_____ Medium in dollars

_____ Medium in personnel

_____ Large in dollars

_____ Large in personnel

(Note: Establish your own criteria for size in each category, since you are the one who will be making the selection.)

I would like to work within the following fields of interest ranked in order of preference:

_____

_____

_____

_____

I would like to specialize in the following career area(s) ranked in order of preference:

_____

_____

_____

_____

I am interested in the following geographical areas ranked in order of preference:

_____ New England	_____ Plains states
_____ Middle Atlantic	_____ Southwest
_____ Southeast	_____ Northwest
_____ Central north	_____ West Coast
_____ Central south	_____ Non–United States _____

(describe)

INTERVIEW FOR INFORMATION

Others' views are also important ways to gain input about any organization or field. Seek out friends and associates who may have information that can help you. You can even call upon people you may not know but whose names you have seen in print and whose views are attractive to you. Some may turn you down, but on balance, it is a good way to get information that may not be available elsewhere.

You may want to speak with accountants, stockbrokers, bankers, and others who may have access to the kind of information you need. With an inquiring approach and a well-planned list of two or three questions, you will be amazed at how often you can get people to share their knowledge with you.

When you do talk with others, you will want to limit your use of their time to questions to which they are likely to know the answers or on which they have sound views. Here are some of the questions you might want to consider. As I have said frequently when providing such lists, these are only thought-starters. By all means, expand the list to include the questions that you feel would elicit the most useful information for your particular needs.

About the Field:

- How does this field look right now?
- What are the long-range prospects?
- Is this a good field to try to get into at the moment?
- Are organizations in this field hiring or scaling down?
- What specific career areas are likely to be hot?
- What do the field's opportunities stem from?
- What seems to be the problem?

About the Employer:

- What are the company's long- and short-range outlooks?
- Where do you see this company headed?
- Where are its opportunities? What are its problems?
- What is its turnover like?
- How would you describe the organization's climate?

About a Specific Individual

- What kind of leader is Sylvia Bradley, the CEO?
- What can you tell me about her style?
- What does her track record show?
- How would you describe her?
- Would *you* want to work for her?

PEOPLE IN THE KNOW

Also try to speak with people who have worked in the particular field and those who have worked for the employers you want to know about. When you talk with them, be sure to keep the door open for follow-up calls. Later, when you have scheduled interviews, you may want to speak with them again.

You would be especially fortunate if your contacts included people who have worked in the department that would be most likely to hire you or in the offices of the city where you would be working. Even better would be to speak with individuals who have reported directly to those for whom you would be working.

Advantages of Seeking Information

Although you will need to be prudent in your use of it, the technique that follows can help you connect in the job market even before you send out a letter or résumé. It is related to the technique of interviewing for information. Here's how it works:

As you develop your list of people to call for information, create a list of heads of departments within organizations where you might like to work. Call each of these individuals; give your name; and say you are calling because you believe he or she may be able to help you by answering a question or two. You will have prepared some key questions, being careful to choose only those that will elicit an enthusiastic response.

If the people you call are in your area, ask if you might stop by for a few minutes to chat about the questions. Emphasize that you are not applying for a job. The odds are good that you will be welcomed. After all, you're not asking to be hired: You're appealing to that person's desire to help others, and you are complimenting him or her by asking for help.

When you meet, get your questions answered and make a favorable impression. Before you close, and only then, ask if you may leave a copy of your résumé *in case your contact happens to hear of any openings that fit your background.* Invariably the answer will be yes and you will have taken two positive steps: You will have provided more information about yourself ("just in case"), and you will have said, in yet another way, that you value your informant as an individual who is well connected.

The odds are good that your name will often come up when someone either inside or outside the organization mentions job openings to this person in the near future. It's one way to gain access to jobs that are filled without advertisements ever being run in the newspapers. I have worked with executives who received major invitations to interview for employment from such initial contacts.

4
Packaging the "Product"

You will need to develop three tools at this stage: a résumé, a cover letter, and a direct-marketing letter. If you have carried out the assignments in the preceding chapters, you are ready for this step. If not, you will save time if you go back through the chapters and develop the necessary information now.

Once you have this material in hand, consider what you want to *offer,* not what you want someone to give you. Come up with a brief phrase that describes what you would like to do with the rest of your career. Make it neither too specific nor too general.

Your Offering Statement

This is a somewhat different approach from that which you may be accustomed to seeing and using or from what you may have read about. Instead of saying what you are looking for, get the reader's attention by saying what you are offering him or her. You might, for example, say "seven years experience in" and then summarize your strongest functional areas.

Keep in mind that what you offer in your statement must match what this employer may want to buy. If you list five functions and don't mention the one the employer has in mind, you reduce your chances of being hired. Whatever you want to do for that employer has to be in your offering statement. And you have to show elsewhere in the résumé that you are qualified to do it even if you are changing careers.

For example, if I were developing an offering statement for myself,

I would not use the word "teach," nor would I use the phrase "government-testimony coaching." The first is too broad; the second, too narrow. Instead, I might say "coach people at all levels in all aspects of presenting information and responding to questions."

That statement defines what I do and what I would like to continue to do throughout my career. Note that I said "coach" rather than "help," which would not have been specific enough. Note also that I said "at all levels" rather than "executives," which would have been too limiting.

Examine the resource materials you have developed to describe your own background and objectives. Review such questions as Who am I? Where am I headed? What do I want to do with the rest of my career? and Where do I want to do it?

If you have difficulty formulating the phrase, you might go back to the part of your "retirement speech" in which you say what you hope to be most remembered for. Reflect on that for a moment. It should either describe what you want to be doing or get you thinking in that direction.

Your offering statement replaces the traditional seeking entry. Remember that potential employers are not nearly as interested in what *you* want as in what you can do for *them*.

Résumés

You have clearly defined your strongest selling statement, the lead paragraph of your résumé. You may also want to include it in your letters. It might not appeal to everyone, but if you tried to write it more generally, you could end up with something so vague it would appeal to no one.

Now you can consider the rest of your résumé. As you develop your résumé by following one of the formats described here, consider how you can highlight your supervisory skills, your task-oriented skills, and your people skills. Essentially, there are only three types of résumés, plus a composite format, that executives and managers need to know about; they are the chronological, the achievements, and the functional.

CHRONOLOGICAL FORMAT
In the chronological format, the emphasis is on the sequence in which you did things, which makes your employers, functions, and accomplishments subordinate. In reverse calendar order, it lists all the positions you've held, starting with your most recent one.

This format is generally chosen by people who have held no more than five major career positions and whose chronology shows a series of advancements or promotions throughout their careers.

If you decide to use the chronological format, but your former titles are not particularly impressive, here's a variation that may help you: Where the format calls for highest title achieved, don't record your title. Instead, write down your responsibilities and describe how you met them. Underscore the words that describe your functions. Allow them to substitute for a title.

Although the chronological form is traditional for résumés, it may not be your choice if you have held a number of positions, some of them for two years or less. It is also not necessarily best for individuals at managerial and executive levels for several reasons: It is dull. It doesn't sell. It fails to emphasize values. With its focus on dates, it tends to downplay your supervisory skills, your accomplishments, and your ability to work well with others.

ACHIEVEMENTS FORMAT

The achievements-oriented résumé is most useful to those who can document major accomplishments on the job or who have outstanding achievements to their credit, particularly when the chronological format would offer no special benefits or advantages. When you develop an achievements résumé, you emphasize your accomplishments and subordinate the where and when. Make certain your résumé does not limit you in the eyes of potential employers by giving undue weight to the *context* of your achievements. If there is a risk that an achievements résumé might portray you too narrowly, describe each achievement in a way that will show how it could apply to a broader area.

FUNCTIONAL FORMAT

In a functional type of résumé, you describe what you do well and would like to continue to do. You might want to use this format when your chronology of employment would not show you to your best advantage, as when you had too many jobs, held the jobs too briefly, or had employment gaps you would rather not explain in the résumé itself.

The functional résumé helps to showcase the *kinds* of things a candidate can do. It is especially useful when the position requires someone to be skilled in several functional areas. Be sure to describe each function in terms of your supervisory, task-oriented, and people skills.

Use the functional résumé if you have strong skills in your field. If,

(Chronological Resume)

Maribelle Marven
1400 Lyndwood Circle
Menvitt, NY 20055

(308) 555-2442

OFFERING:

Solid skills in designing marketing materials, such as booklets and brochures, and in coordinating both creative staff and outside services. Teamwork-oriented, with a respect for deadlines, product quality, and budgets.

YEARS	EMPLOYER	TITLE (HIGHEST ACHIEVED)
1985-present	Brightness Corporation	Senior Projects Coordinator

Supervise the development of marketing materials, including booklets, brochures, direct-marketing letters, and related materials.

1984-1985	InterDesign Services	Marketing Services Manager

Headed a marketing support group responsible for all printed materials related to the sales of clients' products and services.

1980-1984	Barreen Corporation	Graphics Illustrator

Designed and illustrated booklets, brochures, and other printed materials.

1978-1980	The Creative Group	Design Services Assistant

Assisted with all production details related to the design and development of graphics and publications for the firm's clients.

```
PROFESSIONAL MEMBERSHIPS AND RELATED ACTIVITIES:

The Graphics Designers Guild
Marketers of Marketing
Institute of Graphic Illustrators

PERSONAL DATA:

Married. Two children.
Degrees Held:  Certificate, Perkins School of Graphics
               Design
               B.S. Degree, Harrington College
Languages:  Fluent Spanish

AVAILABILITY OF REFERENCES:

References from appropriate sources will be provided
during a personal interview.
```

for example, you are in the public relations field and are strong in financial relations, press relations, program development, and technical communications, you have four strong functional areas—specific areas of performance within your career specialty—to list in your résumé. Review the worksheets you developed in the preceding chapters and record the information for your own field.

The functional résumé is particularly useful to someone whose accomplishments are not easily demonstrated on paper. It is a positive way to put the emphasis on capabilities and job functions rather than on years in a position or on measurable achievements on the job.

COMPOSITE FORMAT

The ideal résumé would, of course, combine a diversity of functional skills, stellar achievements, and a solid chronology, but that is not realistic for most people. Executives and managers who have either strong functional skills or solid achievements, but not both, may benefit from the composite résumé. It is also a good format if you are changing fields because it enables you to feature broad skills, varied employment experience, and the specific functions you have performed. If that is your situation, consider combining your functional skills and your achievements to make both more appealing.

The composite résumé must be tailored to the individual according

(Achievements Resume)

Maribelle Marven
1400 Lyndwood Circle
Menvitt, NY 20055

(308) 555-2442

OFFERING:

Solid skills in designing marketing materials, such as
booklets and brochures, and in coordinating both creative
staff and outside services. Teamwork-oriented, with a
respect for deadlines, product quality, and budgets.

ACHIEVEMENTS:

* Supervised the development of the marketing materials,
including booklets, brochures, direct-marketing
letters, and related materials, that led to the
successful licensing of the Z-BART Unit for PetEx
Corporation.

* Designed and coordinated the marketing materials that
helped to facilitate the successful marketing of a
multimillion-dollar unit that has contributed
significantly to a better environment.

* Supervised the development of the marketing materials,
including booklets, brochures, direct-marketing
letters, and related materials, for three international
campaigns, as marketing manager of a design firm.

* Received the Silver Stylus award at the annual meeting
of the Graphics Designers Guild in 1987.

* Received the Centerfold Award for foldout graphics in
the annual "Oscars of the Graphics Industry" competition
in 1982.

* Contributed measurably to the success of several
products and programs and brought favorable recognition
to my employers.

* Coordinated the efforts of more than a dozen staff designers and illustrators to bring a major project to fruition, on time and on budget, despite major obstacles.

* Reduced printing costs within the organization significantly by coordinating and integrating efforts that previously had resulted in both omissions and overlapping.

EMPLOYMENT RECORD:

YEARS	EMPLOYER	TITLE (HIGHEST ACHIEVED)
1985-present	Brightness Corporation	Senior Projects Coordinator

Supervise the development of marketing materials, including booklets, brochures, direct-marketing letters, and related materials.

1984-1985	InterDesign Services	Marketing Services Manager

Headed a marketing support group responsible for all printed materials related to the sales of clients' products and services.

1980-1984	Barreen Corporation	Graphics Illustrator

Designed and illustrated booklets, brochures, and other printed materials.

1978-1980	The Creative Group	Design Services Assistant

Assisted with all production details related to the design and development of graphics and publications for the firm's clients.

PROFESSIONAL MEMBERSHIPS AND RELATED ACTIVITIES:

The Graphics Designers Guild
Marketers of Marketing
Institute of Graphic Illustrators

```
PERSONAL DATA:


Married.  Two children.
Degrees Held:  Certificate, Perkins School of Graphics
               Design
               B.S. Degree, Harrington College
Languages:  Fluent Spanish

AVAILABILITY OF REFERENCES:

References from appropriate sources will be provided
during a personal interview.
```

to his or her specific needs, problems, and interests. For example, it might emphasize the functional format but include specific accomplishments in connection with or contributions toward the success of the company. Another composite résumé might feature the chronology but focus on the tasks performed.

The Functional Format in Detail

Since you are reading this book, you may be at a time in your career when you want to consider the functionally oriented résumé (or a composite form emphasizing function) as your choice. Let's consider the functional format in more detail.

Looking at the sample provided, you already know that the offering statement sets the stage for all that follows. You can list the functions by category in a single column or in two columns if you have several you wish to highlight. Within this block, you want to highlight up front as many functional skills as possible.

The offering statement provides the focus, but the Types of Functions provides potential employers with a broader selection from which to choose. Again, the more inclusively you can describe your functional listings, the more likely you are to be considered for an interview.

Under the Significant Achievements heading, avoid listing specific employers by date. Doing so might call attention to certain jobs or to a chronology that raises questions.

The functional résumé enables you to present your skills in the best possible way without calling undue attention to chronology, but, if you

(Functional Resume)

Maribelle Marven
1400 Lyndwood Circle
Menvitt, NY 20055

(308) 555-2442

OFFERING:

Solid skills in coordinating creative and outside
graphics artists and designers to meet deadlines and
budgets while maintaining high product quality and
interpersonal relations.

FUNCTIONS PERFORMED:

  Supervisory -- Staff, outside services, budget.
  Managerial   -- Cost control, profit improvement, job
                  simplification.
  Professional -- Commercial art and design for a broad
                  range of printed materials.

ACHIEVEMENTS:

* Supervised the development of the marketing materials,
including booklets, brochures, direct-marketing
letters, and related materials, that led to the
successful licensing of the Z-BART Unit for PetEx
Corporation.

* Designed and coordinated the marketing materials that
helped to facilitate the successful marketing of a
multimillion-dollar unit that has contributed
significantly to a better environment.

* Supervised the development of the marketing materials,
including booklets, brochures, direct-marketing
letters, and related materials, for three international
campaigns, as marketing manager of a design firm.

* Received the Silver Stylus award at the annual meeting
of the Graphics Designers Guild in 1987.

* Received the Centerfold Award for foldout graphics in the annual "Oscars of the Graphics Industry" competition in 1982.

* Contributed measurably to the success of several products and programs and brought favorable recognition to my employers.

* Coordinated the efforts of more than a dozen staff designers and illustrators to bring a major project to fruition, on time and on budget, despite major obstacles.

* Reduced printing costs within the organization significantly by coordinating and integrating efforts that previously had resulted in both omissions and overlapping.

EMPLOYMENT RECORD:

Senior Projects Coordinator, Brightness Corporation. 1985-present
Marketing Services Manager, InterDesign Services. 1984-1985
Graphics Illustrator, Barreen Corporation. 1980-1982
Design Services Assistant, The Creative Group. 1978-1980

PROFESSIONAL MEMBERSHIPS AND RELATED ACTIVITIES:

The Graphics Designers Guild
Marketers of Marketing
Institute of Graphic Illustrators

PERSONAL DATA:

Married. Two children.
Degrees Held: Certificate, Perkins School of Graphics
              Design
              B.S. Degree, Harrington College
Languages: Fluent Spanish

AVAILABILITY OF REFERENCES:

References from appropriate sources will be provided during a personal interview.

(Composite Format: Emphasizing Chronology and Focusing on Achievements)

Maribelle Marven
1400 Lyndwood Circle
Menvitt, NY 20055

(308) 555-2442

OFFERING:

Solid skills in designing marketing materials, such as booklets and brochures, and in coordinating both creative staff and outside services. Teamwork-oriented, with a respect for deadlines, product quality, and budgets.

QUALIFICATIONS:

YEARS	EMPLOYER	TITLE (HIGHEST ACHIEVED)
1985-present	Brightness Corporation	Senior Projects Coordinator

Supervised the development of the marketing materials, including booklets, brochures, direct-marketing letters, and related materials, that led to the successful licensing of the Z-BART Unit for PetEx Corporation.

Coordinated the efforts of more than a dozen staff designers and illustrators to bring a major project to fruition, on time and on budget, despite major obstacles.

Received the Silver Stylus award at the annual meeting of the Graphics Designers Guild in 1987.

1984-1985	InterDesign Services	Marketing Services Manager

Designed and coordinated the marketing materials that helped to facilitate the successful marketing of a multimillion-dollar unit that has contributed significantly to a better environment.

Supervised the development of the marketing materials, including booklets, brochures, direct-marketing letters, and related materials, for three international campaigns.

| 1980-1984 | Barreen Corporation | Graphics Illustrator |

Received the Centerfold Award for foldout graphics in the annual "Oscars of the Graphics Industry" competition in 1982.

YEARS	EMPLOYER	TITLE (HIGHEST ACHIEVED)
1978-1980	The Creative Group	Design Services Assistant

Contributed measurably to the success of several products and programs and received favorable recognition for my work.

Helped reduce printing costs within the organization significantly by coordinating and integrating efforts that previously had resulted in both omissions and overlapping.

PROFESSIONAL MEMBERSHIPS AND RELATED ACTIVITIES:

The Graphics Designers Guild
Marketers of Marketing
Institute of Graphic Illustrators

PERSONAL DATA:

Married. Two children.
Degrees Held: Certificate, Perkins School of Graphics
               Design
               B.S. Degree, Harrington College
Languages: Fluent Spanish

AVAILABILITY OF REFERENCES:

References from appropriate sources will be provided during a personal interview.

feel your employment dates need it, you can put further explanation in a footnote on the second (last) page.

The education section of the résumé is self-explanatory. If you don't have a college degree but have earned college credits, list the courses. If you didn't go to college, list your high school and the years attended. If you have taken special courses within your career field but did not go to college, list the courses.

Generally, if you have a degree, you should list the institution from which you received it. There may, however, be special reasons for listing another institution. For example, if you received your bachelor of science in art from one school but earned credits that are more relevant to the job opening from another institution, you may want to list that school first.

For example, Jane held a bachelor of arts degree in music but supervised a department that designed computer programs. She had earned 12 credits from a leading school specializing in that field. By following the above suggestion, she was able to flag her more relevant experience for her potential employer and still show that she held a college degree.

In the Employment Record, you list the positions you have held. If you have been employed in a number of organizations, you might have to stress within the interview that multiple positions have given you a special kind of flexibility and diversity in dealing with people, or opportunities to gain experience in a wide variety of functional or even geographical areas. When you record the information, simply list years rather than months and years unless you had more than one position in the same year.

When you focus on functions, you also deter the potential employer from the temptation to play calendar arithmetic to calculate your age. The functional format also enables you to skim over less relevant experiences with such statements as "During the interim, I held positions in an unrelated field." Not only is that acceptable; it can also arouse potential employers' curiosity about what you did in the unrelated field.

In the section on Availability of References, never list the references by name, and never give your references' names over the phone. References are among your most valuable possessions in a job search. If you use them up with curiosity seekers, you are not going to have them for long.

One candidate's references happened to include the chairman of the board of a major insurance company, and you can imagine what could have happened if "chairman of the board of a leading insurance company" had been on the candidate's résumé. If several people called the CEO before jobs were even offered, he or she would get rather tired of saying good things about the candidate.

Save your references for when you know you are in the home stretch. I have hired many people, and I have concluded that a candidate doesn't list references who will say anything negative. So if I do check on a candidate, it may be just to verify what he or she wrote on the résumé or said during the interview.

If you visit an employment agency and are asked to fill out application forms that call for references, write "available upon completion of interview with prospective employer" or something similar. If asked, explain why you did this. They're *your* references.

If the employer asks you to list references on a form before you are interviewed, you might want to be a bit more circumspect, but it is still acceptable to write something such as "outstanding [if true] references available from previous employer." Once again, however, I have found that previous employers may not be willing to speak negatively about a candidate, even one who was fired. To get negative information from a former employer requires tactful questioning.

If the employer's form asks why you left your previous employer and you have a legitimate explanation, give it. Valid reasons for being terminated include economic crunch, the phasing out of your job or a department or division, a consolidation, or a bankruptcy. There are other valid reasons for having been let go, but you might be well advised to discuss them during the interview. Just say as much on the form.

Speaking of forms, if an employment form asks whether the employer may contact your present employer, and your present employer doesn't know you are looking elsewhere, write NO in big letters in the appropriate place on the form. Then add: "Contact me *only* at [phone number]." If appropriate, you can add that you would be pleased to discuss this further during an interview. Both agencies and potential employers will understand your need to keep your search private, but you must make that very clear so the person who processes such forms doesn't slip up and make the call. Workshop participants tell me this is an especially high risk when dealing with personnel agencies.

Another scary thing that could happen to your résumé once it gets into the hands of a personnel agency is that it could be sent routinely, and indiscriminately, to people in other companies who know your boss. If you contact agencies, emphasize that your résumé is to go *nowhere* without your express permission, and permit it to go to only one employer at a time.

The Best References

What kinds of people make the best references? People who know you, who know your abilities, or for whom you have performed well. People with whom you have a good relationship. People with whom you would feel comfortable in their home or yours. You can also seek references from other fields if they have some contact with your own field.

It may also pay for you to seek out the unusual, the authority, the noteworthy, the figurehead as a reference. In approaching a politician you should emphasize his or her being a legislator or an elected official rather than one who runs for political office. Candidates aren't good references, but winners might be.

It will help your cause if your references know your work, have worked with you, have supervised you, or have worked for you.

QUESTIONABLE REFERENCES

Friends and relatives are not necessarily good references, nor are people to whom you have been selling or who have been selling to you. In both cases, the potential employer may merely consider the source and discount the references.

SEEKING REFERENCES

Before you give people as references, call them and ask if they would be willing to help you in that way. If you call the right people, explain your situation, and let them know what you expect them to say, most will agree to help you.

Immediately after each interview in which you have given an individual's name as a reference, fill that person in on the content of the interview and what a caller is likely to ask. This is more than a courtesy; it is a way to ensure that your reference says the right things about you.

If your present or former employer agrees to serve as a reference, it may be worth your time and trouble to have a trusted (and skilled) associate call the employer to check on what is likely to be said about you. When I was developing my *Employment Search Program*™, I did this for some of my friends. During a call, I first said who I was and where I was employed. Then I named the person who had been talking with me about employment and asked whether my listener might allow me a few minutes to ask some questions. A few whom I called declined; others wisely asked if they could call *me* back (a good but not foolproof way to make sure the person checking references is legitimate). Others were willing to talk—often in glowing terms. At an appropriate point, I would say: "I know we both want to see Jack hired into a position where your reference will prove to be a valid barometer of his future here. Since his success on the job is important to us, I wonder if you can give me some of your personal observations on where he might function best. That would help me to determine just how successful Jack might be in this position—based on your own observations, of course." Then later, you might press further: "You've mentioned a number of Jack's strong points, but can you tell me a bit about where he might not do as well, so we can avoid putting him in situations where he would be likely to fail?"

Quite often the responses were so revealing that the colleague for whom I was making the call decided to delete the employer as a reference. It's an approach you might want to consider in checking your own references, particularly those from your present or previous employer.

Special Situations

Some situations are not addressed by the standard résumé format. Here are the most significant ones that job seekers have raised in my seminars.

Women Returning to the Workforce If you left a career to raise a family and are returning to the workforce, here are two thoughts for you to consider:

1. You may want to address your absence by writing a composite chronological and functional résumé. Simply list the child-rearing years as such within the chronology.

2. If your return to the workforce will involve responsibilities other than those you carried out prior to your absence, you may have to describe the earlier functions more broadly to bridge the gap between past work experience and desired employment. Otherwise, you should be guided by the same advice given all other job seekers.

Career Changers If you have special skills or academic credentials that apply to the area in which you seek employment, highlight them. For example, one of my seminar participants wanted to get out of the drugstore business and had a master's degree in finance. His résumé had to emphasize finance, not drugstores; it had to focus on the master's degree. It had to list all the courses he had taken that would help a potential employer see him in the career he sought. As a drugstore owner, his work involved finances. He had also managed his own investment portfolio. Those points, too, needed highlighting.

Education Many of this book's readers may be considering a move into teaching or some other career in which academic credentials are stressed. For such a change, you will have to emphasize your educational qualifications. You can leave out majors and minors unless you believe they are relevant, and you can omit them if they are *not* relevant.

For example, if you have a bachelor of arts in theater and you are applying for a job in a totally unrelated area, you might simply write "hold a bachelor of arts degree" and leave out the major. When you get into the interview, you can talk about courses you've taken that are relevant to the particular job opening. At that time, if you need to mention that the B.A. is in theater, fine. By then, you've established that you have other, relevant credentials that would be useful to the employer.

If academic achievements, as well as degrees, are important to the employer, your résumé should include such items as honors list, dean's list, grade point average, membership in honor societies, and academic honors bestowed by organizations outside the school.

If you have written a thesis or dissertation that has been published, mention that as well. Are you, or have you been, a candidate for a master's degree or a doctorate? If so, that should also be listed in your résumé.

If you don't have a graduate degree but have completed credits toward it, say so. If you have a master's or doctorate in progress, say that as well, even if you haven't done much toward it for a year or two.

I know of at least one case in which the requirements for the position included a doctorate or a master's with a doctorate in progress. Yet the individual who was hired had only a bachelor's and had done no work toward an advanced degree. She was hired because she was clearly the best candidate for the job.

Travel Gaps If you took time off from your career to travel, you should show how it helped to broaden your experience and background and made you a better employee. Perhaps it gave you the time to decide what you want to do and where you want to do it. Use the opportunity to point out that you are now prepared to put your full efforts into the position you are seeking.

One woman I counseled had done some traveling between jobs and was looking for a position as a writer with a corporation. She developed a rationale for her travel that showed how valuable it would be to her employer to have a writer on staff who had some familiarity with other societies and cultures.

Out of Work If you have been unemployed for a while and need to cover that gap, you might say, "In a difficult market situation for my particular specialty, I have chosen to remain fully involved in my search rather than accept the wrong position." You have no obligation to say whether you have received other offers or, if so, who made them.

Working Part-time If you have been freelancing or working part-time, say so, but the interviewer has no right to know how much you were paid or for whom you were working. Simply say that this is confidential information.

Wrong Achievements Some achievements may not be the type that you want to call to your interviewer's attention. For example, one executive told me that his most significant achievement was that he had worked on the atomic bomb. however, he was seeking a career change because he felt there was no future in bombs. He finally decided that he would downplay the nature of his work and simply emphasize his involvement in a "major government project" in which he "had supervisory responsibility" and "was successful" in "seeing the project through to completion."

Taking Reasonable Credit In some cases, an achievement may be questioned if your role is not clearly defined or if you appear to be taking too much credit. For example, if you supervise an area in which a project was particularly successful, but the success came about as a result of a committee effort, say so. Then let the success of the project speak for itself. If you headed the committee, that is even more to your advantage.

A Final Word on Résumé Content

Having done your homework, you will know your strengths as well as your areas of least strength. You will also have a better idea of the employer's needs. This input will enable you to develop the résumé best suited to you.

Regardless of the format you use, you are simply exercising your right to sell your services in the best way you possibly can. You *should* present yourself at your best. Take that approach and you will discover that more doors are open to you.

It also helps to remember that you can't, in a résumé, tell the employer everything there is to know about you. The job of a résumé is to summarize what you want to say during an interview. Your résumé should include only the information needed in order for the employer to make a reasonable decision to hire you.

Preparing Your Résumé

These tips for preparing your résumé will help make the résumé effective:

- Always type your résumé; never submit a handwritten résumé or one that has been typeset. Just as a handwritten résumé looks unprofessional, so a typeset résumé looks too professional—almost as though job-hunting were your full-time career.
- Use only 8½ by 11–inch bond paper. The weight should be at least 20-pound offset, and the color should be either white or ivory. Don't use stationery with embossing or artwork. The simpler the better. You want to direct the reader's attention to the content, not the paper. That means no distractions.
- For maximum readability, use a new ribbon on your typewriter or printer when you make the final copy of your résumé.
- Check and recheck your résumé for typographical and grammatical errors. You want nothing to count against you.
- Put your name in the upper-right-hand corner of the cover page and the second sheet. On page 1, include your address and your phone number beneath your name. You want your name to remain visible when the prospective employer reads your résumé or clips a routing slip to it when it goes off to others for review.
- When formatting your résumé, leave plenty of room for borders. This white space helps to frame your résumé and make it more attractive.
- Use a telegraphic style in wording your experience. For example, don't write: "I conducted a highly successful meeting for the managers of my department." Edit this down to read: "Conducted highly successful meeting for department managers." In fact, if you can replace "highly successful" with specifics of what you did, you should do so.
- Never include a photo with your résumé unless your face is integral to the position you seek, as in modeling or acting.
- Notice that the suggested statement on references makes no mention of individuals' names. Never list your references by name in your résumé. Treat your references like gold and give the names

only to people who are serious about offering you a job. Otherwise, you run the risk of having all recipients of your résumé call your references and wear out the references' patience and your welcome.

- Never attempt to be cute or devious in your résumé. Just stick to the facts, presented in the best possible light. Neither undervalue nor oversell your achievements. If you have done your advance preparation thoroughly, you will have no difficulty assembling a résumé that will move the right employer to call you in for an interview.
- Mail your résumé flat rather than fold it. An unfolded résumé is neater, and it makes a better first impression on the potential employer.

No Résumé

There are some advantages to conveying the idea that you do not have a résumé at all. A sound alternative is to prepare an official biography that you can have printed on your current organization's stationery. Such a document communicates status and conveys a greater air of stability than a résumé can. Further, you would not want a potential employer to perceive your résumé as a permanent document, whereas a biography can and perhaps should be perceived that way. You can have a biography typeset and printed, which will give you a neater, more professional piece for your prospects. As noted earlier, there are good reasons not to print your résumé.

Letter Forwarding Your Résumé

Sending your résumé by mail is generally not a good idea. It gives away the store by telling the potential employer too much on the one hand and too little on the other. Your shining hour can come across as only a bunch of words. Since résumés are used primarily to exclude rather than include, the potential employer may rule you out without ever knowing the most important part of you: your personality.

However, you may find yourself in a situation in which it would be inadvisable to decline to send a résumé. An example is when a potential employer in another state asks you to send a résumé after having had a productive phone conversation with you. If that happens, use the sample provided and follow this format:

1400 Lyndwood Circle
Menvitt, NY 20055

July 14, 1991

Roberto P. Damiano
Marketing Support Manager
Marketing Department
Telesort Production Corporation
P.O. Box 31991
Missingly, KS 47502

Dear Mr. Damiano:

   If you are contemplating personnel changes of any kind,
perhaps you will want to consider how someone with my
background might fit into your plans.

   Whether you seek the skills of a generalist or those of
a specialist, my background may suggest possibilities
that you would like to pursue further.

   Please take a moment to look over the enclosed résumé
and consider those areas you might like to explore in more
detail.

   Your call would be welcomed and would not imply any
further obligation on your part. In fact, I would be
pleased to provide you with additional information.

                                        Sincerely,

                                        Maribelle Marven

MM: st
Enclosure: Résumé

1. Address. Also include the date you typed the letter.
2. Heading. Recipient's name, title, department, organization, street, city, state, and zip code.
3. Salutation. Generally use Dear Mr. or Ms. So-and-so, followed by a colon. Use only the last name, unless you are on a first-name basis.
4. Attention. In this paragraph you try to say enough to entice the reader to continue with your letter. You don't want to call attention to your résumé yet, or the recipient may set your letter aside.
5. Interest. Here you try to relate your background to the potential employer's staffing needs.
6. Desire. Your goal here is to stimulate the reader to look at your résumé and then invite you in for an interview.
7. Action. Here you suggest what you want the reader to do: Look at the résumé and schedule an interview.
8. Closing. Use "Sincerely,".
9. Your signature. Type your full name below it.
10. Enclosure. Type in the word "Résumé."

A BETTER LETTER

Avoid the cover letter–résumé approach if you can. In the next chapter, you will learn how to write a letter that will open doors to the hidden job market referred to in many books.

*E*MPLOYMENT *S*EARCH *P*ROGRAM™: ACTION WORDS THAT WORK

Several years ago, the participants in one of my *E*mployment *S*earch *P*rograms™ at The New School for Social Research developed a list of "selling words" they felt would be most useful in preparing résumés and direct-marketing letters. In printing this list, with a few later additions, I thank them for their efforts, which are now helping others.

Ability	Combined	Discovered	Formalized
Accepted	Commanded	Displayed	Formed
Accompanied	Communicated	Diversity	Formulated
Accord	Completed	Doubled	Founded
Achieved	Composed		
Acquired	Comprehensive	Earned	Gave
Acted	Conceived	Economic	Generated
Active	Concerted	Educated	Governed
Addressed	Conducted	Effected	Graduated
Administered	Confidence	Effective	Guided
Adopted	Conscientious	Efficient	
Advanced	Constructed	Employed	Handled
Advantage	Controlled	Enacted	Harmony
Advised	Converted	Encouraged	Headed
Affected	Cooperated	Energy	Helpful
Ambition	Coordinated	Engineered	Hired
Analyzed	Counseled	Enhanced	Honest
Applied	Created	Enthusiasm	Honor
Appreciate		Evaluated	Humor
Approval	Decided	Exceeded	
Aspire	Dedicated	Excellence	Identified
Arranged	Defined	Exceptional	Imagination
Assembled	Delegated	Exclusive	Implemented
Assisted	Delivered	Executed	Improved
Attained	Demonstrated	Exhibited	Improvised
Attended	Dependable	Expanded	Increased
	Designed	Expedite	Induced
Budgeted	Detailed	Experience	Influenced
Built	Determined		Informed
	Developed	Facilitated	Ingenuity
Capable	Devised	Finalized	Integrity
Clarified	Directed	Financed	Initiated
Collaborated		Forecast	Innovated

Inspired
Installed
Instructed
Insured
Integrated
Intensified
Interpreted
Invented
Investigated

Judgment
Justified

Keyed
Keynoted

Lasting
Launched
Lead
Learned
Licensed
Located
Loyal

Maintained
Managed
Manufactured
Marketed
Mastered
Mediated
Merit
Monitored

Named
Negotiated
Nominated
Normalized
Noteworthy

Obtained
Observed

Offered
Officiated
Operated
Opportunity
Ordered
Organized
Oriented Profit
Goal
Orchestrated
Originated
Overcame

Paid
Participated
Perceived
Perfected
Performed
Permanent
Persuaded
Piloted
Pioneered
Placed
Planned
Pleased
Popular
Practical
Praise
Prepared
Presented
Presided
Prestige
Procured
Produced
Proficient
Progress
Promoted
Prompted
Proposed

Proved
Published
Punctual
Purchased

Qualified
Quality

Raised
Reasonable
Received
Recognition
Recommended
Reconciled
Recruited
Reduced
Regulated
Related
Reliable
Renegotiated
Reorganized
Reported
Represented
Researched
Resolved
Responsible
Restored
Reversed

Satisfied
Saved
Scheduled
Secured
Selected
Served
Simplified
Sincerity
Solved
Sparked

Stability
Staffed
Stimulated
Structured
Substantial
Succeeded
Superior
Supervised
Supplied

Taught
Thorough
Thoughtful
Timely
Tolerant
Trained
Transferred
Transformed
Trebled
Trimmed

Understanding
Undertaking
Unified
United
Upgraded
Useful

Valued
Various
Verified
Vision
Vital
Vivid

Wisdom
Won
Worked
Wrote

5
Approaching the Market

Over the past decade, many books and articles on how to succeed in the job market have been written. Yet, despite the sound advice that has appeared in print, thousands of executives, including many who have successfully organized million-dollar tasks, still go about the job search process in nonproductive ways. As a result, they waste valuable weeks, even months, and expend vital energy in ways that are often fruitless. Only when they have become thoroughly anxious and frustrated, and sometimes filled with a sense of despair, do they seek a better way.

Save your energy and your self-esteem. Approach your search as though you were launching a valuable product (which you are) and need to sell it quickly to the right buyer (which you do).

If you have prepared yourself according to the guidelines of the preceding chapters, you are well ahead of others in the market. Most will have started looking before they were prepared and will have bombed out in any number of interviews because lack of preparation weighed heavily against them. Now, without question, many who are still in the market have grown wiser and are doing the homework they should have done *before* they started interviewing. Proper planning is an investment, not an expense.

Employers Also Have Problems

It's ironic that many employers with managerial openings express *their* frustration with the recruitment and hiring system. They say it is often difficult to find the right person to fill an open position. First, *they* are screened out by all those who don't want to work in their geographic areas. Next, they are often forced to exclude all potential candidates except those who have specific knowledge of a particular industry or field. They are also forced to exclude candidates for whom the offered salary ranges are not appropriate. As though that were not enough, they have to exclude candidates who lack the specific kinds of experience or credentials required.

When employers advertise for candidates to fill an open position, they often receive a rash of résumés from people who fail to meet specific requirements that may not have appeared in the ad. When they turn to personnel agencies, their experience is often similar, even with agencies that specialize in the industry or profession.

THE ROOTS OF THE PROBLEM

Why is that so? Why do both sides of the sale have difficulty in making a good match? The employer has little alternative but to continue with the traditional approach to finding the right people. The candidates, on the other hand, have this to their advantage: They know they're looking; the employer doesn't. The employer can speak with them only if they let the employer know they are available.

Thus, responding to an employer's often fruitless efforts to find candidates merely feeds into a system that hasn't worked well from the outset. It's not the best way to handle the problem. As a consultant, if I want to sell you my services and you haven't heard about my organization, it would make little sense for me to wait until you ran an ad or contacted a third party to tell me you are trying to find someone who offers my services. So why should this approach work for a job hunter?

Consultants know that clients rarely announce an available assignment to the outside world. When the initial contact is made, even the client may not have decided that there is a need for services. Thus, people in other departments—especially service departments such as personnel and purchasing—are certainly not going to know about them. Frequently, if they are brought in at all, they become involved after the fact—after the agreement has been made.

Consultants gain most of their client assignments through direct contact: by using a combination of referrals, direct mail, and phone calls. And so should you. In fact, the only *right* way to find a job at the executive or managerial level is to let people—the right people—know you are offering your services. You're not looking to flip hamburgers at a fast-food chain, honorable though that task may be. You need a different approach to job hunting.

Yet, despite the logic of what we have just considered, executives still persist in selling their services in the wrong ways. Here, ranked according to amount of time spent, are the ways by which the majority of people at this level went about looking for a job before contacting me:

- Asking friends and acquaintances if they have an opening
- Calling on employment agencies and search firms
- Contacting placement services provided by professional associations
- Responding to newspaper ads
- Seeking out counseling services
- Writing ads about themselves
- Using direct mail

How Most Executives Approach the Job Market
(Ranked by time expended)

1. Contact friends
2. Register with agencies and search firms
3. Respond to advertisements
4. Contact professional associations
5. Seek out special help groups
6. Hire career-counseling services
7. Run advertisements about self
8. Use direct-marketing techniques

How Executives Should Approach the Job Market
(Ranked by success. Multiple entries for a single number are equally successful.)

1. Market directly.
2. Contact colleagues.
3. Respond to advertisements.
   Register with personnel agencies.
   Contact executive recruiters.
4. Explore professional associations.
   Explore special help groups.
5. Advertise services as a consultant.
6. Use career-counseling services.
   (Should be used in extreme cases only.)

This does not mean you shouldn't talk with your personal contacts, register with employment agencies, let executive search firms know of your availability, contact professional associations, or respond to advertisements in newspapers and trade publications. There is always the off chance that one of those contacts may produce a job for you. However, don't sit back and wait for it to happen: You will use your time better by conducting a direct-marketing campaign. When you follow the traditional routine for job seeking, you may encounter the pitfalls and opportunities described in the following sections.

Personal Contacts

Don't count on your friends having job openings for you or even knowing about them. Because they know you, they may be willing to arrange appointments with you if you request them, but only for that reason. If they sense that you are looking for help in finding a job, both you and they may feel uncomfortable.

If they have nothing and know of nothing, they will have to let you down. Many personal contacts don't know how to do this very well. If you're not careful, they may begin a "daisy chain." Paul sends you to Sylvia, who is willing to see you because of her connection with Paul. Sylvia has nothing, but she passes you along to Brenda, who sends you to Harry. Many cups of coffee later, you will be no better off than when you started, and you will have lost valuable time.

If you want to use personal contacts, use them wisely. Ask them the information-gathering questions raised in Chapter 3 or ask them to review your résumé. Better yet, give them a list of questions and ask them to role-play a potential employer and interview you.

Employment Agencies

For most job-seeking executives, employment agencies are another waste of time. You will spend hours waiting to see a "counselor," who may well envy your past salary. You will fill out countless forms and applications. You will be promised a follow-up call and may not receive one. You may follow up with such agencies yourself only to find that your counselor is "no longer with the firm" and you are back to square one. This is not a productive approach.

If you want to register with agencies, pick only those that have demonstrated a knowledge of your field and that have a strong presence among employers in that field. To register, ask an agency to send you its forms so you can fill them out comfortably and at your leisure, not in a waiting room where you have to balance a clipboard on your lap and are perhaps in the company of some of life's sadder cases. Get the name of a principal of the firm who is likely to be there a few weeks later. Mail your résumé and a cover letter to that individual. Follow through with a single call in about a week. Then forget about it. The agency and your contact may already have done the same. Let's move on to a related source that usually functions in a different manner.

Search Firms

Search firms pride themselves on finding rather than on being found. If you want them, it seems, they may not want you. Rarely do candidates walk through their doors uninvited and walk out with appointments with their clients. Their searches are often so specific that only a chosen few are contacted at the firm's initiative. And "chosen" is an accurate word for what frequently takes place. Many employers and firms have already identified the candidates they have in mind before contacts are made, and quite often the candidates have no idea that they are targets. Often the search firm begins by asking the candidate to suggest "others who might qualify."

To get the attention of search firms, first know the right ones and then appear to ignore them, conveying that you have no interest in an employment change. If they perceive you as needing a job, they are most assuredly not going to take much interest.

Professional Associations

Frequently the organizations that represent your field have placement services. Some are better than others. If you must conduct your search in confidence, don't contact them. Not all of them are irresponsible, but I would be wary of the potential for gossip among people in such positions. On the other hand, you might find them of some value either as your grapevine or as additional sources of information.

Advertisements

Most ads are vague and describe jobs that are hard to fill, often with employers that have difficulties recruiting for a wide variety of reasons. If the job is easy to fill, why has it reached the advertising stage? If it is not easy to fill, you may well wonder why. Salary, location, and reputation for turnover are just a few of the reasons you may find when you have an interview with an employer you found through a recruitment ad in a newspaper. Remember that most of the good jobs are gone before they ever find their way into advertisements.

Even ads that name the organization are fraught with pitfalls. (Don't waste your time on an ad that asks you to send your life history to a box number.) Employment ads tell you little but ask for much. In return for a few teasers by way of job description, they may ask for not only your résumé but also your salary requirements. The odds are strong that the information you provide will be used to screen you out rather than to invite you in.

If you feel compelled to respond to a help-wanted ad, here is the only approach to take: Read the ad thoroughly two or three times. Jot down the points that it makes. Observe the sequence in which the points appear. Then follow the advertiser's formula in writing your reply. Take this ad, for example:

```
EXECUTIVE MANAGER WANTED
Diversified Fortune 500 company in
high-technology field has opening
for manager with 3-5 years'
information processing experience.
Must have demonstrated sound
ability to supervise and present
technical reports. Should
have strong managerial skills as
well as an ability to carry out
research, analysis, program
development, and implementation.
Headquarters city location. Submit
résumé and salary requirements in
strictest confidence [indeed!] to
Box X340X, this newspaper.
```

ANALYSIS

Point by point, in sequence, what does this ad say? What are the buzz-words? Jot them down and prepare to respond to them in sequence in your reply, assuming that you feel reasonably confident that you won't be replying to an ad for your own job.

Here's how the text of your reply might look:

Dear Boxholder:

I read your ad for an executive manager in the May 3 *Miami Herald*. If you are looking for someone who can work at the Fortune 500 level in high technology and has 3–5 years' information processing experience, I believe that my credentials will be of interest to you.

I have a solid record of demonstrating a sound ability to supervise and to present technical reports. I have strong managerial skills and can carry out my own research, analysis, program development, and project implementation.

I would be pleased to provide a résumé and discuss salary at the time of a personal interview.

Sincerely,

Paul Alexander

COMMENTS

They have given away nothing, and neither have you. Sure it's a game, and you are trying to beat them at it. Unfortunately, they play it more frequently than you ever will. Is it worth your time? Not likely. But if you insist on trying, without giving them everything they need to rule you out without even seeing you, this is the best way to do it.

Special Help Groups

Some people, particularly the chronically unemployed, find special help groups such as Forty Plus and therapy groups to be beneficial. However, you may be asked to come up with some money for the use of their services, and you may even be asked to devote as much as a day or two a week to help staff what may be a volunteer effort for most of the people there. You might want to look elsewhere.

Career-Counseling Services

Don't look to career-counseling services, however. I have a strong bias against anyone who takes my money, uses my time, expects me to do most of the work, and delivers so little in return. It is possible to pay thousands of dollars to such a firm, complete its cycle, and be even less certain of who you are or where you want to spend the rest of your career. (That, of course, is one of the few things such firms promise to help you decide.)

Advertising Yourself

When you run ads about yourself, most of your replies will come from people who want to sell you something. Forget such ads unless you want to offer your services as a consultant—perhaps as a way to get through the door in the hope of finding a job without looking for one. Even then, don't expect your phone to ring off the hook. As you will recall, consultants employ a different strategy.

Direct Marketing

Now we are down to the winner. This is the marketing tool that will get you in for an interview before anyone other than the employer knows there may even be an opening. As you saw earlier, it is even possible for your approach to *create* the awareness of a need.

We'll explore the direct-marketing approach in the next chapter, when you will develop the tools to sell your services.

What's Out There

Rarely will you know at the start of a search what job opportunities might be available, which reminds me of the adage children hear so often: You never know until you try. After all, if you write to a potential employer, you may discover something you may not have considered:

Jobs become available for a multitude of reasons, some of which are known only to the person who will ultimately make the hiring decision. Perhaps the department is being expanded. Perhaps a new and necessary function has been identified. Perhaps someone is considering early retirement. Perhaps a reorganization is imminent. Perhaps someone is going to be let go.

You see, there are many possibilities that could lead to opportunities for you. This is particularly true when you are already in the door with an announcement that your skills and experience might be available to the employer.

A Word of Caution

In the meantime, don't make the classic mistakes. Don't call on the wrong people. Don't wear out your welcome. Don't exhaust your references. Don't complain to anyone other than the professionals whose job it may be to listen. In fact, although it makes all the sense in the world to confide in your spouse, be careful not to lean too heavily. A spouse who can keep the old chin up now may be more willing and able to let you draw on his or her energy reserves during trying moments later on.

Instead of taking a hit-or-miss approach, take the time now to prepare yourself properly. That may keep you out of the job market for a few days or even a week or more, but it will give you the time you need to prepare yourself fully for the most important task: surviving the employment interview.

6
Building Your Job Leads

It might sound like work, but a good salesperson knows a lot about each prospect before making contact. A typical organization requires new salespeople to know the following before making a call:

- An overview of the prospect's business, including products or services.
- A detailed knowledge of the department in which the salesperson's products or services might be needed.
- A working knowledge of the key people in the organization.
- A thorough profile of the head of the department that would be likely to use the products or services being offered.
- Information on at least one current activity of consequence within the organization and preferably within the department.
- An awareness of a specific need for the products or services being offered.
- The skills to convert the salesperson's products or services into benefits that the prospect will find attractive.
- An inquiring mind and an ability to listen *actively*.

Your Research

It doesn't matter whether the market is up or down or whether your particular field is growing or shrinking. You need a job, and no matter what the employment situation or the economy looks like, you have to go about it with your full energy. Forget "buyer's market" and "seller's market." It is neither one nor the other, because nine out of ten jobs at management levels are never even advertised.

Even the amount of display advertising in the employment section of a major newspaper has little bearing on how easy it will be for you to find a job and get hired. Lots of ads merely mean that there are lots of employers who have jobs they have not been able to fill without resorting to expensive measures. These are not necessarily good employers, nor are the jobs necessarily good ones. They are just jobs—and they may not even be right for you.

If lots of jobs are advertised, does that mean you should sit back and wait for an employer to call you? If few jobs are advertised, does that mean you should give up?

Since most good jobs never reach the newspaper, you have to go out and find them, and you won't find them by looking in all the traditional places and ways. Salespeople don't wait for customers to advertise that they are looking for products and services: They develop their own prospects lists, and they learn as much about those prospects as they can before they make their calls.

There are many directories that can help you do this. You can either compile your own information or hire someone to do it for you. Don't worry about getting outdated information when you retain an outside source. Any list will be out of date the minute you prepare it, no matter who develops it.

LIST HOUSES

If you can afford to do so, consider retaining someone who can develop a list based on the criteria you established during the earlier exercises. List houses are sometimes helpful; you can find them in the Yellow Pages. You need only tell a list house what information you need from the following categories:

- Types of employers by field of endeavor
- Which department heads you want, by name and title
- Your area of specialty
- Geographical area(s) in which you would like to work
- Employer size in dollars and personnel
- Any other criteria you feel are relevant to your search, including phone numbers

DATA BASES

Many list houses now have data bases that enable them to sort information quickly and at relatively low cost. Start locally, but be prepared to go to major cities to find the right firm. Keep calling until you find the one who can help you.

Some firms have minimums and will be reluctant to sell you fewer than a certain number of names. So when you negotiate with them, you may have to let them know that you are willing to pay on an hourly basis if your target list turns out to be smaller than their requirements.

PRINCIPAL SOURCES

In most cases, a list house will use the same sources you would use if you were developing your own lists. The following list names the principal sources and explains what they do.

- *The Business Periodicals Index* lists the publications that serve each individual field.
- *The Directory of Directories* provides the names of all directories in print.
- *Gale's Encyclopedia of Associations* maintains listings on more than 1000 associations that might lead you to additional prospects.
- *Gale's Encyclopedia of Business Information Sources* enables you to locate a wealth of resources that provide information on business.
- *The Guide to American Directories* offers information on more than 3000 directories and nearly 500 topics.
- Moody's manuals divide U.S. industries into five categories and analyze each one.
- *The Standard Rate & Data Business Publications Directory* lists publications by topic in nearly every field.
- *Statistics Sources* provide statistical data by topic.
- *Thomas' Register of American Manufacturers* provides extensive, in-depth listings on manufacturers, trade boards, chambers of commerce, and more.

PRINTOUTS

Don't ask for the lists on labels; get printouts. That will be cheaper, and you are probably going to transfer the data into your computer anyhow. On the other hand, if the list house can provide you with floppy disks that are compatible with your computer or if it can input the data to your

computer directly through a modem, consider having it do so. The time
you save could be well worth the expense.

MORE ABOUT COMPUTERS

Although we covered this earlier, it bears repeating: If you have a
computer or have access to one, it will save you a tremendous amount
of time during your search. With a computer you can store and update
all your prospect records, generate envelopes, create custom letters and
résumés, and proofread your materials before you print them.

These services can be provided by outside organizations as well, but
you may find that the costs add up quickly—especially if you do your
writing and editing on the firm's time. Consider purchasing your own
computer and taking lessons on it. You may be money ahead in the long
run. If you do purchase, give serious thought to an IBM or a machine
that runs IBM software. As much as I like Apple (and we also have Apple
hardware), I haven't seen any companies marketing Apple clones,
whereas IBM has set the industry standard and, together with third
parties, offers more programs that can be run on more computers. You
would be well advised to keep this in mind when you purchase your own
computer.

CHECKING AGES

The typical executive will prefer to hire someone younger than himself
or herself. Regardless of federal law, this is a fact of life, and any
executive can find lots of rationales for not hiring older applicants. So
face this regrettable certainty and learn the ages of your prospects when
you gather information. Then you can put more emphasis on prospects
who are your age or older.

TIMING

As you develop your research information further and begin to concentrate on your prospect lists, consider this: Studies have shown that many
executives make the greatest number of changes in staff about a year
after they themselves have been hired. If you read last year's membership directory in the field you are exploring and then compare the
member listings against those in the current directory, you can target
some prime prospects quickly.

YOUR NEXT STEP

Armed with your prospect lists, return to your library and consult the
directories that list what has been printed and where. The *Reader's*

Guide to Periodical Literature is a good place to start. Also, many libraries now have computers that allow you to search for articles by topic and by author. Use these resources to search for articles written by or about:

- The department head to whom you will be mailing your marketing letter
- The department head's specialty field
- The organization
- Changes or trends within the industry

Read the articles. Consider what impact each may have on the executive whom you plan to contact. Consider the impact on his or her department. Explore for insights that will tell you more about the personality or style of the individual as well as the organization.

Setting Up Your System

Don't wait until your direct-marketing campaign is in full gear before you develop a way to keep track of your prospects. You want to have a functioning system at your fingertips before the reply calls and letters start coming in. If you have a computer, you should develop a program that will function to the fullest extent your equipment allows. You should have a separate record for each prospect. The ideal would be a mail-merge system that allows you to use the same data base to print addresses on envelopes, create individual or repetitive letters, and keep track of the status of each prospect.

How you do this will be entirely up to you, of course, but at the very least you will need the following:

Records Have a permanent record of the names, titles, organizations, and addresses of every single person to whom you send a letter. If you find that you should be in contact with a different person within any organization, change your records immediately. If you are put in touch with additional people within any organization, add them to your records at once. Keep yourself up to date on this and you will never regret it; fall behind and you may send the wrong letter to the wrong person and put yourself out of the running.

A Card System Develop a prospects card system. If you don't plan to store the information in a computer, you should use 5- by 8-inch index cards. See the boxed illustration.

_____   Date   Action _____
(Name of Organization Prospect)

_____   ____   _____
(Name of Your Contact)   (Sent Letter)

_____   ____   _____
(Address)   (Received Reply)

_____   ____   _____
(Phone Number)   (Asked to Interview)

_____   ____   _____
(Source of This Job Lead)   (Date of Interview)

                                ____   _____
                                       (Person to See)

                                ____   _____
                                       (Notified References)

                                ____   _____
                                       (Sent Add'l Materials)

                                ____   _____
                                       (Had Interview)

                                ____   _____
                                       (Sent Followup Letter)

(Reverse side of card)

• Information about the organization:

• Information about the person to whom you wrote:

• Information about the person who will interview you:

• Specific points that have been raised:

• Questions you want to ask during the interview:

A Standard Letter Develop a standard letter that you can use for your initial mailing. Adapt it to fit special situations or any special information that you are able to get. Send a personalized letter each time.

1400 Lyndwood Circle
Menvitt, NY 20055

July 14, 1991

Charles J. Schmidt
Sales Services Manager
Marketing Communications Department
Vector Licensing Corporation
25 W. Fourth Ave. N.E.
Aldenburgh, PA 30026

Dear Mr. Schmidt:

If your department seeks a professional who has written and supervised the production of award-winning support materials to launch the marketing of a major service effort, you might want to consider how my background may fit in with your needs.

In 1987, I supervised the development of the marketing materials that went into a successful effort to license a multimillion-dollar unit that has significantly reduced the cost of making an important environmental product available to the public. The package booklets, brochures, direct-marketing letters, and other materials received the Silver Stylus award at the annual meeting of the Graphics Designers Guild that year.

This is one of many projects throughout my career in which my work has contributed measurably to the success of a product or program and has brought recognition to my employer. I particularly enjoy coordinating the work of creative staff and outside services to bring about the teamwork needed to meet deadlines successfully with the most professional product possible, and within budget.

> If these skills have a place in your staffing plans now
> or in the near future, I would be pleased to discuss my
> background in more specific detail with you in a personal
> interview.
>
>   Sincerely,
>
>
>   Maribelle Marven
>
> MM: st

Your Direct-Marketing Letter

You want to mail your direct-marketing letter to as many prospects as possible and as quickly as possible. A wait-and-see attitude will only cost you valuable time. If you send out a handful of letters this week and you get no responses right away, how long are you willing to wait before you send out more? Another week? Two more weeks?

What if none of those get responses? And what if you get only one or two responses out of, say, the ten letters you mailed during that period? Will you repeat the process? If so, you are in for an unnecessarily long period of unemployment.

If you researched your market thoroughly, you should have come up with at least one hundred prospective employers. If you mail letters to all of them at the same time, you cut your waiting period significantly.

YOUR LETTER'S FUNCTION
Letters, however, are not intended to bring in job offers. What is their function, then, if not to get you a job? Their purpose is to condition the market, to let your prospects know you are out there. If one or two prospects happen to take the initiative and invite you in for interviews, that's great. It's also the stuff of which dreams are made.

Follow-up

No matter how powerful your letter might be, if you want any real action, you will have to take the next step. You will have to follow up with phone calls to find out what happened to your letter. Make your first calls in about ten days. You may find that any one of the following may have happened to it:

- It may not have been received.
- It may not have been read.
- It may have gone to the wrong person.
- It may have been forwarded to the right person.
- It may even have been forwarded to another *wrong* person.
- The recipient may not have placed you as high on his or her priority list as you would like.
- He or she may be waiting to see whether you follow through on your correspondence.
- There may not be an opening and the recipient felt no obligation to call or write you to let you know that.
- A form letter that promises to "keep your résumé on file" may be on its way to you.

And that doesn't exhaust all the possibilities by any means. The responses may have you making changes on your prospects cards or in the computer. They may have you sending out new letters to different people in the same organizations. They may even have you ready to stop making any more calls.

Perhaps a fear of the unknown—a legitimate concern over what to say when you call—explains why not everyone in every organization works in sales or marketing. Most people are just not cut out for the prospecting task—at least not until they get desperate or lucky. Like it or not, selling is your job for now, so why wait for either desperation or good fortune? Why not act at once?

MAKE THE FOLLOW-UP CALLS

Follow up the leads you have created through the research you have done. Don't excuse delay with the plea that you don't want to receive several calls at once. Don't kid yourself into inaction by saying it's best to avoid interviews with the least desirable employers on your list until you've heard from your prime prospects. If that should happen, by the way, consider yourself very fortunate.

When to Call? If you want to reach the individual directly, call when he or she is most likely to answer the phone—when secretaries and receptionists are least likely to be around. Call 15 minutes before the start of business hours or 15 minutes after the close of the organization's day. If those times don't fit your schedule, call just before lunchtime. You are likely to find your prospective employer just returning from a meeting and preparing to go to lunch. You might also try calling right after the lunch hour. Your prospect may have just a few minutes to spare before heading for another meeting.

Any of the above choices give you the advantage of being able to keep the call brief. That will enable you to avoid being interviewed by phone and thereby lose your opportunity for a face-to-face meeting.

Worst Times Several candidates have told me that the worst times to try to reach a prospective employer are between 10:00 and 11:00 in the morning and between 2:00 and 3:30 in the afternoon. "If it's not meetings, it's something else" was a complaint they shared.

SCHEDULING INTERVIEWS

If you have a miraculous stroke of good luck and several prospects call you for interviews, schedule them at your convenience. If the lower-priority prospects call, at least they are contacting you because they are on your list. If you happen to have interviews with them before the prime prospects come in, you'll still have plenty of time. Most interviews take a week or more to set up, and you rarely get feedback for another week or so—if you hear at all. It isn't as though you have to give an answer overnight.

Should a prospect press for a quick answer, however, you should stall: It is prudent to wonder why the urgency. In fact, you might find a courteous way to ask that very question.

If you do interview with your least desirable prospects and get no offers, consider yourself fortunate in another way: You've gained actual interview practice before your prime prospects invite you to talk with them.

Again, if you're going to do things right, send out all your letters at once. Be done with it. Get your main marketing tool out there and working for you, so you can *get hired*.

PREPARING TO CALL

Armed with the knowledge you need about yourself and your prospect, you can prepare for your follow-up phone calls. Here are some tips that will help you have the right attitude for these calls:

- You will place your calls at reasonable times.
- You have valid reasons for making the calls.
- You are offering, not asking.
- You will be courteous at all times.
- You can always get out of a difficult call with a simple statement expressing your regret at inconveniencing the individual.
- You can put a difficult caller out of your thoughts quickly.
- You can make other calls that will be more productive.

PHONING YOUR PROSPECTS

The people you do reach will be friendly and courteous if you handle the call well. This requires some knowledge of the process and of what to say when the party at the other end answers you. First, however, you will have to get past the receptionist or secretary. Since you know your prospect's name, you already have an edge over anyone else who is trying the same approach but has addressed the letter to "Department Head." (That almost guarantees the letter will be trashed. Misspelling the individual's name comes close. Writing to someone who is no longer with the organization ranks third. Using the wrong title ranks fourth.)

Before you ask to speak with the person to whom you wrote, play it safe. Find out if the person is still with the company and how to pronounce his or her name. How should you do this? Ask the person who answers the phone. If you happen to reach the individual directly, ask for the correct pronunciation of his or her name anyhow, if you are uncertain of it. I have never met anyone who has been offended by having a caller do this.

Once you have established the correct pronunciation of your prospect's name, use it immediately. If it's a difficult name—for example, DeRaeve—do your best. At worst, you'll be corrected, and at best you'll avoid the embarrassment of muttering something like "Well, anyhow . . ." or "Well, whatever. . . ."

Introduce yourself at once. Say your name before you state your business. Everyone likes to know to whom he or she is speaking. Next, state the reason for your call. Forget the pseudo-friendly "How are you today" approach that some books on selling recommend. It wastes your prospect's time. Instead, ask whether he or she has time to speak with you.

Say, "I wrote to you about a week ago and I wonder if this is a good time for you to talk with me for a few moments." No hat-in-hand tones, no hearts-and-flowers monologues. Just a simple, direct inquiry in 5 seconds or less.

If Ms. DeRaeve says she's sorry but she's very busy right now, understand that she probably is. After all, you weren't exactly penciled in on her day's agenda. Respond accordingly.

Say, "I understand. When would be a good time to make a *phone appointment* to speak with you?" Note that you ask to make a "phone appointment." You *don't* ask when would be a good time to call her back. And you certainly don't ask her to call *you* back.

Faced with that decision, she may give you a day and time or ask you to set something up with her secretary. If so, be sure to confirm the appointment by saying that you will look forward to speaking with Ms. DeRaeve again on May 3 at 10:30.

Another person you call, Mr. Brooks, may decide to give you a few moments to make your pitch and then tell you he is sorry but he has nothing for you. That is most apt to happen if you make the mistake of pitching your wares on the phone. You will have better results if you use the same few moments to gain an appointment.

Follow-up calling is often neither easy nor pleasant for the uninitiated. You certainly don't want to blow it by stammering something like "I don't suppose you have any job openings, do you?" This is where your research, planning, and preparation come in. Thanks to the work you have done, you have a much better approach at your fingertips, one that can ease the pain and make this step a bit more pleasant for you.

Say, "Thank you, Mr. Brooks. I wonder if we could set a time to talk about your upcoming expansion. I'm sure your department must have an active part in it. I'd like to learn more about it in any case." Then stop talking and wait for a response.

"In any case," you ask? What do I mean by that? Well, I have found that the phrase is a tipoff to the potential employer that you just may be looking for a job. But even if Brooks has nothing at the moment, he knows you've gone to the trouble to learn about a project in which he is involved.

Not bad for a 5-second opener.

Your prospect's response is difficult for this book to anticipate, but either it will lead to an appointment or it won't. If you don't get the appointment, your alternative goal is to keep the door open. I have known several job seekers who were in for the long haul. Many of them received invitations to interview months after an initial contact just because they kept the door open.

Your follow-through in this case? "I understand, Mr. Brooks. Could you send me some information about your department's role in the project—and perhaps about its other activities? It sounds like an interesting place to be."

That's another 5 seconds, but what a powerful move on your part. You have just created a space that would be difficult for your prospect not to fill. And you have also planted another suggestion with your capper: "an interesting place to be."

Think about it. You have expressed understanding. Not bad. You have kept the focus on your interest in the project. Even better. And you have parlayed that into a request for information—not only about the project but also about the department as a whole. Better yet. Your ending? A seed well planted.

Your prospect is highly unlikely to say no. In fact, job seekers have told me that some prospects have reversed themselves at this point and scheduled either a phone appointment or a visit. So be prepared once again. Have your calendar handy. (You will learn about the best days and times for appointments in a later chapter.)

Since you may not be so fortunate, be prepared to close the conversation before Brooks has time to ask you too many more questions. Suggest that you would be pleased to give your mailing address to his secretary rather than take up any more of his time. Either you will be transferred to the secretary or Brooks may take down the information personally.

Either way, you have done well. You have another reason to follow up, and you have information on which to base a future contact. Keep in mind that this prospect is not in your "hot" file, however. You just want to keep the pot simmering as you devote more attention to other and more likely potential employers.

When They Call You

If your prospective employer calls, he or she may try to reach you at home or at the office. Regardless of where you receive the call, here are some points to keep in mind:

- Most prospective employers will call you at home, and they should, unless you have given them specific permission to reach you at the office. (Suggestions for handling the calls to your office are given at the end of this discussion.)
- Phone calls, by their very nature, are interruptions. You have the right to tell a caller that you are in the middle of something, ask for a name and phone number, and offer to call back within a specified period of time.
- You also have the right to ask what the call is about. No one can be expected to commit to memory the names of everyone to whom letters have been written. If the caller doesn't offer the information and you are not certain whether he or she is one of your prospects, ask.
- Call back. According to some studies, the person who initiates the call has more control over how the call proceeds and the recipient has less say about how and when the call is terminated.
- Keep a note pad handy. Write down the caller's name (even if you have to ask for its spelling), the name of the organization, and the nature of the questions you are asked.
- You too have a right to ask questions. Know ahead of time what you might want to find out during the screening call.
- Keep the conversation short. Don't reveal more than you have to, or you may not be invited to an interview.
- Have your calendar near the phone. You want to sound organized from the start. If you have any activity tentatively scheduled for the suggested date, particularly if it's a function involving your present position, say so and negotiate another date. You don't have to give reasons or excuses; just suggest an alternative date and time. By taking the initiative, you demonstrate another of your managerial skills. You control your own life.

Office Calls   If a call comes to your office and you haven't given prospective employers specific permission to reach you at work, that may tell you something about the caller or the organization. Without your okay, it would be unprofessional to call you at the office. Coworkers may get wind of your search; rumors may begin to circulate; and your job could be put in jeopardy.

If a caller were to try to probe you with interview questions while you were at your office phone, he or she could place you in even further jeopardy. Should that happen, simply say, "I'm not prepared to discuss that at the moment. Could I have your phone number so I can call you at a better time? Four-thirty on Thursday would be good for me. Is it for you?"

Regardless of how you feel about the intrusion, stay calm. The caller's discourtesy, disrespect, and indiscretion reflect on him or her, not on you. So be patient, but remind yourself to check this out in your next conversation—which you will initiate.

THE PURPOSE OF THE CALL

A prospective employer who calls you after receiving your marketing letter will want to screen you further. Your letter has opened the door. Now it's up to you to keep it open and get the interview.

The caller may want to clarify information or gain new information, but you can be sure that one of the objectives will be to learn more about you as a person. At a conscious or subconscious level, your caller will be monitoring your word choices, voice tones, and general attitude. Without eye-to-eye contact, you will have to work a little harder to establish and maintain the rapport you need to get to the interview stage.

Here are some tips that will help:

- Listen carefully and completely.
- Do not interrupt.
- Provide feedback that shows you have clearly understood what the caller said.
- Verify dates, times, and locations if an interview is arranged.
- Respond, don't pitch. Ask, don't sell.

ESTABLISHING RAPPORT

When you are on the phone, try to match the caller's rate of speech. That is one way to establish an early rapport with your caller. Just don't allow yourself to speak so slowly or so rapidly that the rate is uncomfortable for you.

A caller's speech rate can also tell you whether he or she is primarily in a visual, auditory, or kinesthetic (tactile) mode at the moment. Rapid speech generally indicates visual: Try to respond with such phrases as "I see" or "It looks good to me." Moderate speech generally indicates auditory: Use "Sounds good," "I hear what you're saying," and the like. Slow speech usually indicates kinesthetic: Use such word choices as "I'm comfortable with that" or "get in touch with."

Here are some examples of visual, auditory, and kinesthetic words and phrases that might help you in your conversations.

Visual	Auditory	Kinesthetic
Appear	Amplify	Bigger
Clear	Attune	Better
Envision	Call on	Boil it down
Focus	Describe	Come to grips with
Foresee	Ears (I'm all ears.)	Comfortable
Look	Express	Control
Notice	Harmony	Deal with
Observe	Hear	Feel
Obvious	Listen	Get a handle on
Perceive	Loud and clear	Hand
Perspective	Question	Hold
Picture	Sounds good	Produce
Resemble	Talk	Put
See	Tell	Start
Seem	Tune in	Touch (Stay in touch.)
Show	Voice an opinion	
View	Word for word	
Visualize		
Watch		

Voice Tones Monitor your own voice tones as well. Record yourself during other conversations, particularly those that are mildly stressful. Suction-cup attachments for tape recorders are widely available. You don't need permission to make a tape provided you use the recording for no other purposes than your own personal needs.

Here are some problems you might listen for: Do you sound nasal, whiny, bored, indifferent, tense, hostile, or antagonistic? Pompous, arrogant, bombastic? The possibilities are numerous, and no, even your best friends won't tell you. In fact, most of them might not be able to. Without private coaching, you're on your own with this one.

If you think there's a problem, it can't hurt to work on it. Voice and speech control are beyond the scope of this book, but you might try some of the books in the Reading List section. Your voice is an important tool in any field, especially when you're on the phone.

CONTENT OF THE CALL

Once again, the screening call is not a one-way transaction. You too should ask questions, and since you are the one who placed the call, that will be easier to do. This is the time for you to discover what your research could not. Is there a specific opening? How does the position happen to be available? (Is it new? Was it recently vacated? Where is the former occupant?) To whom does the position report? Do others report to the person in the position? How many? What does the position entail? Can you describe the department briefly for me? What kinds of projects is it currently undertaking?

Screening works both ways, and it should. The information you ask the prospective employer to provide will give you the input you need to help both of you to arrive at a good decision. The prospective employer, of course, has the same objective in mind when asking questions. If you *both* decide to go forward with the interview, each of you will have a better basis for your discussion.

If you don't like what you've heard or feel that you wouldn't fit the position well, say so in a gracious way. Don't wait for the prospect to say it for you, and don't waste your time or the prospect's with interviews you know will go nowhere. Your initiative will be respected, and you will gain points for your thoughtfulness in saying why you would prefer not to be considered for the opening. Many executives have told me that this kind of closure has opened doors for them later on: The employer either offered a more relevant position later on or referred the candidate to a contact who had a position open.

After you hang up, reflect on the prospective employer's attitude. Were you treated with dignity and respect? Did you get full and open responses to your questions? Was the person patient and helpful? Jot your observations down on your prospects card.

YOUR NEXT STEP

Once you have your first appointment scheduled—on the right day, at the right time—you're ready for the next step: the Interview.

Part Two
The Employment Interview

7
Preparing for Interviews

Your résumé and phone call will have succeeded if they get you to the interview stage. From the day you set the appointment, consider your interview to be a two-way street. Before either you or your prospect says a word, you will have begun to assess one another and wonder what the other is thinking. That's human nature.

Questions such as Will I like him? and Will she like me? may seem trivial until you go through the process, but they take on a strange significance once you set the date. Yes, there will be some elements of feeling one another out, some aspects of courtship, and, of course, some elements of selling. And each of you will be doing a bit of both.

Here is where you want to walk a fine line. You want to appear neither aggressive nor submissive in this encounter. If your concept of a job interview has overtones of either desperation or hard sell, erase those thoughts now. The most successful attitude you can convey is one of staying in charge of *you*.

Your Attitude

From the moment you first think about it, each meeting is an opportunity to exchange information, a way to see whether the relationship should go further. Fix this firmly in your mind, and the rest will begin to fall into place.

You are there to learn and share, and so is your prospect. Each of you wants to find out more about the other. Your goal should be to help each of you see whether your skills and your prospect's needs are a good match. Provide your prospect with the opportunity to see how you measure up and to show you, in return, how he or she measures up.

You will both want to gather more facts, but you will also want to gather impressions. This is where you have the edge: You can start collecting your impressions of the organization even before you meet the interviewer.

You should also keep in mind that you are there to be sold as much as you are to sell. Be professional at all times.

STRESS LEVELS

When you enter an interview, focus entirely on the other person. That will help keep you from thinking about yourself and becoming self-conscious. Self-consciousness could cause you to communicate feelings of insecurity regardless of how subtly you might try to control them. In fact, trying to control nervousness can cause your attention to turn even further inward. You could become distracted in your efforts to concentrate on the interviewer, causing the process to go even further downhill.

The message? Head up. "Keep your eyeballs off your belly button," as the drill sergeant used to say in boot camp. Direct your total attention toward your interviewer and take in all the information you can, just as quickly as you can absorb it.

When the interview goes right, the potential employer will want to know whether you'll be an asset and you will want to know whether the opening is right for you. The interviewer will be looking for clues about your character, and you will be assessing the interviewer and the company. It's a matter of give and take, with both participants striving to do the appropriate amount of giving and taking.

Interviews need not be highly stressful experiences. Certainly a little stress may be in order, but let's let the cat out of the bag and acknowledge that interviewers can feel anxious too. Unless your field is human resources, it is unlikely that you have done very much interviewing from the employer's side of the desk. That may also hold true for the person who will interview you.

Instead of thinking about putting yourself at ease, you might reframe that thought and consider how you might help make your interviewer feel more comfortable. Then, even if employment interviewing is a relatively unfamiliar experience for each of you, you will be more focused on the other person's feelings than your own.

With stress at a level you can manage, your mind becomes clearer and, in an interview, the dialogue becomes more meaningful. So whether you have gone through dozens of employment interviews or are facing your first one, keep in mind that having a positive perception of what should take place is the first step toward helping it become a reality. Attitude may not be everything but, as the saying goes, "It sure beats whatever is in second place."

What can you expect to happen during the interview? Here is where all your research and planning pay off again. Since most employers are neophytes when it comes to employment interviewing, you can almost call the shots just by being properly prepared. A note of caution, however: This much power carries with it grave responsibilities—and risks.

You have the responsibility to ensure that each of you gains and provides the input the other needs. And you take the risk that your own skills may overwhelm the situation and not give either of you clear and accurate information about the other.

Clichés must have some truth to them, or they would not survive. The one that comes to mind here is: Knowledge is power. And going in, you have far more knowledge about the potential employer than your interviewer could hope to have about you. Most interviewers will not have put as much planning and preparation into the interview as you have. You again have the edge.

There is no question that your homework has given you enough information to keep the interviewer responding to your questions throughout most of the meeting. Having absorbed the information in this book, you will also know how to use skills that will have him or her doing so *enthusiastically.*

In fact, the information provided here could enable you to swamp the interviewer. If you do that, however, both sides will lose because you will leave the meeting without ever having given the interviewer the opportunity to gain the input needed to make the right decision.

The tools you will have at your command when you finish reading this book include "pacing and leading," "embedded commands," "future pacing," and "reframing." You will also learn several techniques for discerning whether the information you receive is valid and comprehensible.

These tools and techniques have existed for centuries; researchers have merely refined and codified them in recent times. Use them to help improve the quality of communications in your life and in the lives of others. Your goal in this environment is to end up with the right job and the right employer. You have an obligation to help ensure that your interviewer ends up with the right employee for the right reasons.

How do you find out what you need to know, such as what your employer will really be like once you are on the job? How do you use the interview to uncover information that would displease you if you learned it only after you were hired?

One job seeker was so anxious to get the job that he accepted a generous salary offer without asking about reporting relationships. Once on the job, he learned that the department setup was such that he had accountability but lacked the authority and supervisory control needed to achieve the department's objectives.

Thus, knowing what to ask and how to get answers can indeed come in handy. We'll cover that in one of the upcoming chapters.

YOUR EMOTIONS

Being factually ready is not enough. Having the information you need and knowing how to ask the right questions are only part of the task. You will also have to know what kinds of emotions you might experience once you walk through the interviewer's door, and what to do about them.

Will you be anxious, nervous? Will this make you appear outwardly excited, overstimulated, and overresponsive? Or will you retreat inwardly and become silent, withdrawn, and defensive? Any of these emotions may result unless you can anticipate them and work to overcome them beforehand.

Whether you are basically an Approach-oriented person or an Avoidance-oriented one is not the issue here, however. Your first concern should be to recognize that any emotions not dealt with beforehand could manifest themselves in ways that would not be conducive to a good impression during the interview or in many other situations.

The simplest solution is to recognize the fine work that has been done in the field of relaxation and that is available in such classic books as Herbert Benson's *The Relaxation Response.* Visualization, in which you imagine yourself being successful in the situation that may cause you stress, is another valid and useful technique. The best treatment on this subject as it might pertain to job seekers can be found in a book by Matthew McKay and Patrick Fanning titled *Self-Esteem,* pages 171 to 189.

Recognize that your emotions are real and your brain must feel they are needed, or they would not exist. Your task is to allow the brain to realize that you are in control and don't need it to set off alarms. Why wait until you are in the interview environment to find out whether this might happen to you? Through your use of relaxation and visualization techniques, you may be able to reduce the possibility of an emotional upset greatly and perhaps eliminate it entirely. Preparation—informational and emotional—is your key to a successful interview.

Your Appearance

Since first impressions are lasting ones, what you have chosen to wear and how it looks will be the first things the interviewer learns about you. Thus, we will discuss your appearance in detail here. There are general rules for interview attire that apply to both women and men who are seeking managerial, executive, and professional positions. A few words that come immediately to mind—and that will be repeated as you read on—are conservative, tasteful, and practical.

Nearly every job in every organization has its dress code. Often the code is unspoken, and a veneer of permissiveness can mislead an applicant. Don't believe what others may be paying lip service to; instead, notice what people in jobs comparable to or higher than yours actually wear.

If you are still uncertain, dress more on the conservative side than flamboyantly or according to what happens to be the current fad. Your clothing should not detract from the desired focus on your professional credentials. Women's styles in business clothing are more flexible now than they were 15 or so years ago, when a mannish look was almost expected of a woman who wanted to get ahead. However, it might be better to gather fashion ideas from *Working Woman* than from *Cosmopolitan.* These tips will help you dress appropriately:

ATTIRE
All clothing should be tailored and businesslike, never revealing. Unless you can afford a new wardrobe every season, avoid faddish colors and styles that might soon become outdated.

Blends of Dacron® or polyester with wool, linen, or cotton wear best in a work environment. They are least likely to show wrinkles, and look the best when worn. Fabrics such as silk and 100 percent polyester tend to cling and call undue attention to themselves. Avoid most leathers and suedes, because the tend to ride up. Ultrasuede™ is an exception.

Blouses and shirts should complement your suit and should also be conservative—either solids or simple patterns. Avoid sheer fabrics. A blend of cotton and polyester or Dacron® tends to wear best.

Women have several options provided they remain within the code. They can wear suits, dresses, coordinates, skirts and blazers or, if tasteful, skirts and blouses. Avoid slacks and pantsuits. If you choose to wear a sweater, make certain it has a businesslike look. A skirt should reach slightly below the knees when you stand so you are appropriately modest when you sit—even in a low or deep chair.

Men need to wear suits even though dressy blazers may be acceptable once you are hired. Although vests can be attractive, keep in mind that they tend to make people look heavier. Forget leisure suits, even if they do happen to be in style.

Men's trousers should be long enough to break slightly at the crease. Men should wear long-sleeved shirts even if every other man is wearing short-sleeved ones. For a first appearance, sleeves look better than hairy arms—or even wrists, since you should be wearing a jacket (barring a temperature of more than 80 degrees in the office, of course).

Fabrics A blend of worsted and synthetic fabric will hold up best under most circumstances. Stay away from 100 percent polyester and other all-synthetics. Shirts and blouses should be conservative. For men, oxfords and button-downs convey a traditional look and remain in style. Your tie or scarf should be made of 100 percent silk, period.

Color and Patterns Wear the lighter shades in warm weather, the darker in cold weather. Muted pinstripes, herringbones, and checks are acceptable.

Women should choose neutral colors such as navy and other blues, black, all shades of brown, and the full spectrum of grays. Stay away from bright reds and greens, yellows, or oranges.

Men should select one of the broad spectrum of blues or grays. Browns tend to rank low in status in men's clothing, and greens are out of the question. Suits may be solid, muted pinstripe, subtle plaid, or a small check or herringbone.

Shirts and blouses can be white, pastel blue, or cream. Solids and pinstripes are generally appropriate for most business situations. Accessories should generally be pale blue or gray, with burgundy ties, scarves, or shawls (if tasteful). Ties and scarves can be solid, paisley, striped, or patterned, but they should be conservative and they should complement your overall appearance. Subdued patterns are appropriate for both men and women.

Shoes Men should wear black shoes. Women's shoes can be black, brown, burgundy, or any other color that accessorizes well with their outfits—lighter shades are appropriate in warm weather. White or patent leather (black) may also be appropriate, depending upon the season and locale. Avoid trendy colors and patterns in footwear.

Your shoes should be made of leather. They should be conservative and should reflect good taste. Men should pay particular attention to whether their peers and superiors generally wear dress slip-ons, lace-ups, solids, or wing tips.

Women should avoid overly high heels. Their shoes should be closed at the toe and heel regardless of the season or the current fashion. Some executives look askance at people who would run through mud and slush in semibare feet. Which makes another point: Wear appropriate boots or rubbers over your shoes in bad weather.

Hosiery Men should wear socks high enough to keep their legs from being exposed when they sit with their legs crossed. Women's stockings should be sheer, seamless, and in solid skin tones—no patterns. Women would be wise to carry extra stockings to avoid appearing in public with runs.

Jewelry Keep jewelry and other adornments simple and in good taste. Wear nothing that dangles, flashes, or might otherwise distract an interviewer or call attention to itself. Use few pieces—one ring per hand—and wear the highest quality that would be appropriate in a business setting. Do not wear items that identify you with fraternal or other organizations. Avoid cufflinks even if they happen to be in style. Some people regard them as affectatious for office wear.

Accessories Your accessories, such as briefcase and pen, must be of top quality. Never carry plastic pens or pocket liners for pens. For women, an accent scarf, if conservative, can be an attractive accessory when worn correctly. Briefcases should be made of leather, reflect top quality, and have an executive look. Don't wear sunglasses or lenses that darken in bright light. People must see your eyes if they are to believe you.

Women's purses should be made of leather and should coordinate with their shoes. Keep purses small but functional. Although debates continue over whether to carry a purse if you are carrying a briefcase, here's the practical side of the matter: Women's business clothing does not have as many pockets as men's clothing has. You'll probably want to carry both a purse and your briefcase. Just be sure you can carry both comfortably.

Regarding the cliché question of "How do you shake hands if both your hands have something in them?" either sling your purse over your shoulder or set your briefcase down. You might also leave your purse in a secure place with the receptionist before you go into the interview.

LOOKING YOUR BEST

What you wear is extremely important, but *how* you wear it can make the difference between a great first impression and a bomb. Here are several keys to looking your best in what you wear:

- Carry nothing in your jacket, skirt, or trouser pockets. Bulges are not attractive, and people under stress tend to fidget with items in their pockets.
- Never take your suit jacket off unless you absolutely must. When you're trying to make a good first impression, it can weaken your executive image.
- Have all buttons, hooks, and snaps in place and secured properly.
- If you have been traveling, change to a fresh shirt or blouse before the interview. If your clothing is wrinkled or rumpled, either change it or use a portable steamer for quick touch-ups.
- Your clothes must fit well. Nothing mars a first impression more quickly than bulges. If you are overweight, have your clothes tailored to fit.
- Adjust your tie or scarf properly *before* you walk into the reception area.

GROOMING

There are several personal matters to consider if your first impression is going to be as positive as it needs to be. These tips will help you complete the look:

- Your clothes must look as though they just came from the cleaners.
- Check to see that your hair is neatly combed or brushed. Scissors or hairspray used discreetly in a restroom can take care of that wisp of flyaway hair that won't stay down at the last minute. Use an unscented spray.

   Women can have their hair done before an interview but should not experiment with a new hairdo. Men should *not* get a new haircut within 3 days of an interview unless they get just a light trim. On the other hand, men should never appear to need a haircut. Beards or mustaches must also be well-trimmed.
- The heels and soles of your shoes must not appear worn, and the uppers must be well polished.
- Your nails must be neatly manicured. Polish colors should be muted. Makeup should be appropriate for daytime wear. Cologne or aftershave also should be subdued.

- Try to schedule your interview in the morning, before a new beard growth overshadows your appearance or makeup begins to fade. If you must interview after midday, you should shave again if you're a man and reapply makeup if you're a woman.
- Carry breath mints or sprays, and use them appropriately.
- If you know that you look your best before the interview, you will reduce your stress levels considerably.

HOW AND WHAT TO EAT

Eat a high-protein breakfast. Take a multivitamin tablet or caplet. Take a B-complex vitamin. Do whatever you can to help your body get the nourishment it needs to put forth its best effort. An interview takes a lot of energy; have some reserves so the experience doesn't drain you.

Avoid heavy, starchy, or carbohydrate-laden foods before an interview. They tend to let you down shortly after you eat them. Also avoid any foods with excessive roughage. Natural cereals, whole-grain muffins, nuts, and berries can stick in the throat and pose problems when you interview.

Your Voice

Job seekers sometimes experience fatigue and stress, which can bring on allergies or colds. Don't wait for this to happen to remind yourself that you need to stay and sound healthy if you are going to do well during your interviews.

If you need to reduce the symptoms of a cold, allergy, hayfever, or sinus condition, avoid medications that contain antihistamines unless they are absolutely essential. They can dry you out. Use products that will help keep your throat moist. Avoid alcohol-based products. This is not the time for a brandy cure for your cold, and alcoholic beverages won't help you get the job.

Stress also takes its toll on your vocal cords, so monitor your thoughts and actions at all times. Do whatever will be most helpful—and healthful—to you in taking the edge off your reaction to the stressful events you encounter, particularly during a job search.

If you get into the interview and find that nervous tension or a cold has left you with a dry throat, use a glycerine-based cough drop. If you don't have one, you may be able to produce some moisture by nipping the tip of your tongue between your teeth and by thinking of sucking on a juicy lemon just as you nip your tongue. If you are having more serious difficulties, ask for a glass of water. No harm will come of doing so. If the interviewer is a smoker and the smoke is giving you problems, let him or her know this. Most people are considerate.

SPEAKING FOR SUCCESS

Speech incorporates a number of tools that can add interest and contribute to a successful interview; they include range, volume, pace, rate, intensity, inflection, and even pauses. Enunciation and pronunciation are still others. Here are some brief tips that can help you use your voice well:

Range Speak within a range that is comfortable for you. Don't try to talk in a low voice just because you've heard that doing so conveys authority. That would create strain, making you sound even less authoritative.

Volume Speak loudly enough to be heard clearly, but support your voice with air from your diaphragm.

Pace Your rate of speech should match the interviewer's as closely as possible for better rapport, but don't speak either too rapidly or too slowly. Speak at a moderate rate of about 125 to 150 words per minute. Vary your rate from time to time so your speech doesn't become monotonous.

Diction Good diction also is important. Try to pronounce all the parts of each word you use, especially words ending in "ing." You'll leave a better impression with your interviewer.

Static Avoid sounds, words, and phrases that interfere with communication; these include "it's like," "you know," and "okay" as well as filler sounds such as "uh," "and," or "and, uh." They occur most frequently when people are tired, ill-prepared, or under stress of some other kind. If you catch yourself using them, relax and focus your mind straight ahead to your next thought. Avoid filling gaps with any of these words or sounds by saying nothing until you are ready to use the next "real" word. Your interviewer will never notice the pause.

How to Get the Right Kind of Rest

Get a good night's sleep before your interview. If you aren't feeling well, even a brief rest an hour before you head to the interview can do wonders. It will give you a chance to relax and clear your mind of any excessive stress. That should help you concentrate better during your meeting.

If you have difficulty falling asleep the night before an interview, drink a glass of warm milk. Warming the milk releases chemicals that can help the brain relax. You can also do light stretching exercises and take a hot shower just before going to bed.

Make sure your self-talk is positive. Don't tell yourself, "I can't sleep." Instead, say, "I have done my best. I have prepared myself for the interview. Now I'm feeling very relaxed; my eyes are growing heavy. I can feel my head, my arms, my legs, and all of my body slowly easing, relaxing deeper and deeper into the bed as I let go and enjoy a comfortable, restful sleep." As you say this, match your words to your breathing rate, slowing down more and more with each affirmation.

PROGRESSIVE RELAXATION
You can also relax each part of your body progressively. Start with your toes. Tense them and then allow them to relax as you tell yourself that your toes are now relaxed. Do this with all the muscles in your legs. Next, focus on the tips of your fingers and work your way back until you reach your chest. Now shift your focus to the muscles in your buttocks, then to the small of your back, and gradually work up your spine. When you reach your shoulders, switch to the top of your head and work your way down through all your facial muscles (eyes, ears, nose, mouth, and jaw). Move to your neck and shoulders and follow the same procedure.

If you are still awake, your last step is to tense every single muscle in your body all at once and then let go slowly. As you release, make a mental picture of anything you find tranquil and peaceful. Hold that image and tell yourself that you are sinking warmly, deeply, and pleasantly into total relaxation.

Who Might Interview You

You are likely to meet with people from three different departments during your interviews.

Head of Human Resources This person may interview you more for input about your attitudes and aptitudes than to learn about your skills. He, let's say it is, may not make the decision to hire, but he may have almost any degree of influence depending upon the organization. His department will also be responsible for briefing you on such things as benefits and organizational policies and procedures.

Your Supervisor This is the person to whom you would report.

Needless to say, he or she will be making the final decision to hire. Both of you should get to know each other well during the interview.

Other Interviewers Some organizations may arrange to have you meet with others with whom you would be working. Some of these contacts may be arranged to give you a better feel for the work environment; others may be selected for the boss's perception of their acuity in sizing up people. About the only cue you can rely on to determine which is which is to notice whether the contact tells you about things (to give you a better sense of the environment) or asks you about things (to size you up).

As long as you are given the opportunity to meet these people one-on-one, you will need no special preparation. However, if you are scheduled to meet several people in one interview, you will need to refer to the techniques for group interviews that are discussed later in this book.

What Interviewers Seek

What will the interviewer look for in you? It bears repeating: First impressions are lasting ones, and your persona will be established by the appearance you present. That includes your attire, your grooming, your demeanor, your voice tones, and your body language. You, of course, should be using the same criteria to evaluate your interviewer.

Rehearsal Techniques

There are several ways to prepare yourself for your upcoming interview. All of them have been tested, and all of them work. However, you may personally be more comfortable with some than with others.

VISUALIZING
To prepare themselves mentally, successful athletes visualize themselves going through every aspect of whatever their events require. For example, high jumpers see themselves taking every step of their approach, leaving the ground, going over the bar cleanly, and landing properly in the pit.

Visualizing begins with identifying and sequencing all the steps. If you can visualize yourself going through every step of the interview, you will increase your chances of success even more. Here's one theory on why this may work: Your subconscious mind receives the input and, not knowing what is real and what isn't, processes the information as though you had already been successful. Your anticipation of success becomes easier to fulfill. You will read about the specific aspects of interviews in future chapters. Become familiar with all of them and rehearse them before your interview.

RECORD YOUR REHEARSAL

At the very least, you will want to review the questions and the suggested ways to respond to them that appear in Chapters 14 through 17. There you will learn about the areas of questioning, the questions asked most frequently, the types of questions that are asked, and the techniques you can use for responding.

In writing, describe a position that might interest you. You don't have to be perfectly qualified for it, just interested in it, but be realistic. Be as detailed as possible; list duties, reporting relationships, and anything else you can put on paper.

Now list the questions that you feel would be most likely to come up in an interview for this job. Sequence isn't important right now. You can organize the questions into categories, levels of difficulty, and styles of questioning, or list them at random.

Next, find a quiet area where you can concentrate totally. Read one question into a tape recorder; stop the tape; and think about your answer for a moment. If you are not certain how to respond, turn to the appropriate section of this book and look up the suggested strategy for handling the question. Then record your reply while using the strategies that you will be reading about later on.

Go to the next question and do the same thing. Continue this way for no more than 15 minutes, which should come out to about a dozen questions. That is about as much as you want to attempt at one time if you are to gain maximum benefit from your rehearsal without becoming distracted.

Play back your tape. Listen carefully to your responses. Did you answer the question appropriately? Did you relate your response to the job at hand? How did you sound? Were your voice tones friendly, cooperative, and enthusiastic? Do you sound like the kind of person the employer would hire? Would you want to hire yourself?

Try yourself out on even the most unusual questions you can conjure up. You want to use these rehearsals to prepare yourself to deal comfortably with anything that interviewers may throw at you.

ROLE-PLAYING YOUR REHEARSAL

You should also practice answering questions with another person asking them. Have a colleague play the part of an employment interviewer. This will give you the practice you need before you go to the appointment. Although it helps to visualize this aspect of interviews beforehand, it can be even more beneficial to act out your plans physically. The face-to-face interplay that comes with these sessions will give both you and your colleague opportunities to evaluate the way you handle other kinds of situations. For example, the "interviewer" might choose to misinterpret your responses, follow up your replies with loaded questions, or use other techniques described in Chapter 15. Rehearsals can also give you the opportunity to see how well you handle the opening and closing portions of the interview.

Be sure to audiotape these practice sessions, and videotape them if you can. When you review them with your colleague, ask for a candid evaluation. Listen from the employer's perspective; focus not on what you did "wrong," but on where you could do better next time. If you experienced a particular difficulty with any aspect of this role-play session, take a break, identify the problem, refer to this book for ways to handle it, and then try again.

Your body language and voice tones will probably diminish in these rehearsals, so exaggerate them a little. It's a useful technique, because if you overdo them in practice, they'll come out just about right in the actual interviews. Keep in mind that learning is a process that goes best when you take it in small steps and in short sessions. Create a checklist such as the one on page 102, or make copies of that one. Use a clean sheet for each rehearsal.

Rehearsal Checklist

After each role-play, have your "interviewer" evaluate you according to the criteria below. Use the scale provided.

1	= needs considerable work
2, 3	= needs some work
4, 5, 6	= passable, but. . . .
7, 8	= good
9	= very good
10	= outstanding

	1	*2 3*	*4 5 6*	*7 8*	*9*	*10*

Stage One

- Overall greeting
- Handshake
- Smile
- Body language
- Eye contact
- Voice tones

Stage Two

- Gestures
- Posture
- Eye contact
- Attitude
- General content
- Responsiveness to:
    Type of question
    Technique for asking
    Interviewer's attitude

Stage Three

- Picked up closing signals
- Responded properly to:
    Verbal signals
    Nonverbal signals
- Used proper closing techniques
- Handshake
- Smile
- Body language
- Eye contact
- Voice tones

When You Should Interview

If possible, avoid interviewing on Mondays and Fridays. It is difficult to hold the attention of people who are just getting back into the work

YOUR INTERVIEW CHECKLIST

Research on the Organization

Financial

- I have read the current annual and quarterly reports.
- I know their major products and services.
- I know their sales and profit figures.

Locations

- I know their major plant and office locations.

Key issues

- I have reviewed general trade publications and know the major stories about this organization that have appeared in the past six months to a year.
- I know the topics that are hot in this particular industry at the moment.

People

- I have looked up their executives in the various registers.

General

- I have obtained as much information as possible from the organization itself: general literature about the company, a description of the department that is hiring, and a description of the job that is open.

Personal Preparation

- I have listed my questions in a handy place.
- I know exactly how to get to the meeting place.
- I know the pronunciations of the names of people who will interview me.
- My clothes are cleaned and pressed. All buttons are in place. Shoes are shined. Hair is trimmed and neat. Nails are clipped and clean.
- Briefcase, pad, and pen are ready.
- Extra résumés are in a manila folder or envelope.
- Complete information on references is typed neatly on a separate sheet.

routine or trying to wrap things up for the weekend. Tuesdays are like a fresh start, since all of Monday's catch-up work should be out of the way by then. Thursdays are also good because enough of the week has passed that the interviewer may be looking for a change of pace. Wednesdays seem to be neutral.

After lunch, people's digestive systems take oxygen away from the brain, so afternoons also can be ruled out. That leaves Tuesday and Thursday mornings as the best times for interviews, with Tuesday gaining a slight edge because it leaves you with more of the week for phone follow-ups if needed.

Ten o'clock seems to be about the best time. It gives the interviewer time to check mail and get any paperwork and phone calls out of the way. It also gives you at least an hour before both parties begin to get hungry and possibly lose concentration. Also, many executives have coffee at about ten, and you might catch them in a more relaxed, sociable mood.

8
The Three Parts
of an Interview

Interview formats differ with the styles of the persons who conduct the interviews. Some will be structured; others will be free-flowing with open-ended questions such as "What do you know about this job?" Some interviewers will be helpful and will take time to put you at ease as you try to respond to their questions. Others will be more aggressive and may challenge whatever you say. Some will be calm, poised, and in control. Others may be nervous and apprehensive, and you may have to help *them* if you want to have a productive interview. All employment interviews, however, go through three stages:

Saying Hello

This is the social amenities part of the interview. Usually, you and the interviewer will talk about such general topics as whether you had a good trip coming in, whether the directions given you were all right, whether you found the office or building without difficulty, and the weather. Don't be misled by the seemingly trivial nature of the dialogue. People tend to go through a sizing-up stage in any relationship. Researchers tell us it has to do with the syndrome they call fight-or-flight, expressed best by such unspoken questions as, "Is this contact going to be threatening to me in any way?" "Does anything about this contact suggest that I will need to run, attack, or protect myself?"

Of course, in most human contacts—especially in an office environment—the fight-or-flight syndrome does not weigh as heavily as it might in other situations. Say, for example, you were to find yourself suddenly confronted by a stranger at night in an empty bus or train depot. Your fight-or-flight receptors might then be very sensitive. Of course, most employment interviews will be nonthreatening experiences in nonhostile environments. Nonetheless, the sizing up will take place—and by both parties.

Whenever two people come together, especially for the first time, they begin absorbing sensory input about one another before either has said a word. Thus, your first minute of the interview may be the most important of the entire meeting. We will cover body language, eye contact, and voice tones later.

The social amenities part of the interview also enables both of you to settle down and clear the butterflies that each of you may well be experiencing. After all, your interviewer is probably not trained in screening candidates and may feel some stress over asking the right question or making the right decision. Your interviewer may also be uncomfortable with meeting new people, causing this feeling-out period to take a little longer than it would with a more seasoned, sociable interviewer.

Setting the Tone

Since it is up to the interviewer to set the tone for the meeting, you can pick up some additional cues by listening to how he or she poses the first question or comment that follows the initial encounter. This may also reveal something about the interviewer's interests or priorities. After all, out of everything the interviewer knows about you, this is the topic being raised first.

For example, an interviewer who says, "I see you worked for *Cosmo*" is making a statement about something that may be of personal interest. If establishing comfort levels is the objective, and it should be, why not help the process along? Instead of launching into a verbal résumé, why not respond with, "Yes, I did. Did you also work there?"

From the use of the nickname, the chances are either that she did or that she knows someone who does. You'll learn that from her response. Follow up whatever she says about her interest in the magazine, but do so in a friendly way. After all, this is just chit-chat, but it can be very important to establishing a positive rapport.

Common ground provides a solid foundation. When it is available to you, use it well. People tend to want to be around those whom they like and to speak highly of them. Sharing an area of mutual interest is an important way to become liked. Of course, there are other important attributes you can display, such as interest, empathy, understanding, and enthusiasm. These too should come out in your early dialogue.

You are there to help the employer determine whether you have skills that can fill the needs of a position. When you can learn what the interviewer wants from you, it will help you do a better job of explaining how you meet the qualifications.

I recall one candidate who interviewed with me several years ago for an opening my employer was anxious to fill. Each time I tried to redirect the conversation toward his ability to juggle several projects at a time, he kept coming back to his experience in a narrow, limited area that was of little interest to us. I gave him several opportunities to learn what he needed to know so he could tailor his responses to what we were seeking. Finally, I had to conclude that he didn't listen well, didn't care, or lacked the skill that we needed most.

Interviewers generally come down to these questions when they make a hiring decision:

- Are the skills right?
- Did the candidate care enough to do his or her homework?
- Is the personality a good fit?
- Are this candidate's goals and objectives appropriate here?
- Can the candidate do the job?
- Is he or she motivated to do the job?
- Will the environment enable this particular candidate to get the job done?

Getting Down to Business

At some point, the two of you will find yourselves ready to settle down and discuss the purpose of the meeting. The interviewer, being more familiar with the physical surroundings, generally relaxes more quickly and moves the interchange from step one to step two.

Frequently, the transition occurs when the interviewer offers you a seat. If you sense that you have completed the social amenities and the interviewer still hasn't offered you a seat, three things may be happening: He or she is uncomfortable, unfamiliar with the process, or wants to see whether you will take the initiative.

In any case, remain cordial. To learn where the interview will be conducted, observe where the interviewer sits. Does the interviewer return to the desk or move over to an area that has a sofa and chairs? Once the interviewer begins to sit down, if you have not been offered a seat, immediately ask: "Would you mind if I sit over here?" Seat yourself in the most comfortable chair available.

Environmental Assessment If the transition does not occur and you both sense that you are frozen in time with nothing to say, you might try a technique I call environmental assessment, which means nothing more than "look around you." As you walk into the office, try to spot anything that expresses the interviewer's personality. It might be a photograph, a certificate, or an award. Look at it purposefully and say something like, *"That's* interesting. It must have some special significance to you. Can you tell me about it?"

One job seeker told me that before an interview with the president of a firm, he learned that he would be lucky if the meeting lasted five minutes. The president had been described as being "tough to get through to." In the first minute of the interview, the candidate experienced what he had been told. The president received him coolly and contributed little toward a feeling of comfort. The candidate seized the reins, looked at an unusual object on the president's bookshelf and said: "How interesting. I'll bet there's a story behind that." He paused. Silence. Then the interviewer smiled and began to tell the story behind the piece.

The ice was broken, and the interview lasted nearly an hour. The president confessed that he often tested new people to see how they would react to stress with clients. Thanks to environmental assessment, the candidate had passed the test and was offered the job. He didn't take it.

Environmental assessment can be used in other ways to help you learn more about situations. More on this in a later chapter.

The Generous Offer

Here we're talking not about salary, but about such matters as being asked if you would like coffee, a cigarette, a drink, and so on. If you want to say no, do so. Don't elaborate; just say "No, thank you." Anything more could damage the rapport you need to build.

If you want to indulge, be careful about what you say. You may find yourself being tested to see whether you are a loner, to see whether you are insensitive to circumstances, or for some other reason. The best response would be, "Only if you're having one." The interviewer may then respond by saying, "No, but why don't you go ahead." If so, your answer should be an unqualified, "No, thank you."

If silence follows, which it might, you may need to move the interview forward yourself. Instead of selling, begin by asking. You might phrase your next line this way: "Perhaps you could tell me a bit more about the position." Then pause. It's the interviewer's turn now.

The Time Line

The business aspect of your interview has officially begun. This part generally takes two-thirds or more of the time the interviewer plans to allot to you, and the final part of the interview takes at most 20 percent of the time (and frequently less).

If saying hello ran three minutes, you can anticipate that you may have about twenty minutes to conduct your business before you begin to say goodbye. This is consistent with the fact that preliminary interviews average about thirty minutes. Don't use the length of the interview as a barometer of success, however. Short interviews can be just as productive as long ones, and the converse is also true. Knowing how much time it took to get started, though, will tell you something about how long the interview will last.

In an employment interview, the average question takes about twenty to thirty seconds to ask and about thirty seconds to answer. The narrative portions of the interview (such as describing the position) generally run about two to three minutes at a clip, and both the interviewer and the candidate will have at least one narrative segment.

The point? Interview time goes by rapidly, and you will be unable to probe any topic in depth. If you have only 20 minutes for business discussion, if you remove six minutes for narrative portions, and if each question and its answer take approximately one minute, you and the interviewer will have time for only fourteen questions and responses before you find yourselves making moves toward closure or departure.

You are looking at fourteen questions, the answers to which may decide a career. How each of you uses the time to showcase your offerings and to learn everything you need to arrive at the best possible decision becomes critical. We will cover that vital information in later chapters. For now, keep in mind that you will have to stay on track and not allow your responses to drift from the point in question. It is never to your advantage to say too much.

Saying Goodbye

Saying goodbye is the final phase of the interview. The signals can be obvious, as when the interviewer rises and says, "Well, thank you for coming in today." or they can be more subtle, as when the interviewer begins straightening up papers on the desk, putting your résumé and letter back into a file folder, or glancing at a watch or clock. Other indications that the meeting is coming to a close include longer pauses between questions and the interviewer's glancing toward the door.

Be perceptive. Some interviewers may not know how to close the meeting, or this may even be a final test. If the interviewer just sits there silently, almost as though meditating, take the initiative and test to see whether it's time to start saying goodbye.

Say something like this: "Well, George, I certainly appreciate the time you've taken to discuss this position with me. It sounds interesting, and I'm sure we'd both like to give it more thought over the next few days. Is there anything else we need to cover?"

This gets both of you over a potentially rough spot in the conversation and leaves the interviewer with the opportunity to either explore other points or help you close the meeting. When you both appear to agree that it's time for you to leave, you will need to know what comes next.

Unless things have gone unusually well, you are unlikely to find yourself negotiating terms by the end of this first meeting. For one thing, few interviewers have or would choose to exercise the sole power to make a hiring decision. If you are offered the job on the spot, you may not want to be too hasty about accepting it anyway. In a half-hour interview, some questions must have been left unanswered, including why the interviewer is that anxious to fill the job. No, regardless of how much you may feel you need the job, give yourself a few days to think about it. You'll be glad you did.

Instead, use this closure time to find out how you did, whether you are still in the running, and how to follow up. Here are some possible scenarios:

1. If you feel the meeting went well, say so, but with relaxed enthusiasm: "I know we both have some questions and other considerations we'll need to explore, but it would seem that we're pretty close in what we're looking for. Would you like me to call you in a few days to see what our next step might be?"

2. If you're not certain how the meeting went, if you think the employer has doubts about your candidacy, or if you have doubts about the position, you might try a slightly different tack, saying simply, "What do you feel our next step should be?"

3. If you aren't interested in the position or feel it's not a good match, you can say that also: "I appreciate your inviting me in today, George, but I'm sure we agree that my background wouldn't be a good match for this particular opening. But I do appreciate the time you've given me. It was very thoughtful of you."

Remember that your voice tones and body language are significant here as well. Remain cordial. Keep the door open for dialogues in the future. A few years back, a candidate who found it necessary to use the not-interested close was called many months later by the same individual. The latter had been impressed by the candidate's sincerity and maturity. Because the job seeker had a specialized background, it was reasonable that she might continue to look for a good match. That possibility led the interviewer to recommend the candidate for a position that opened up in another area of the division. The candidate, as it happened, was pleased to interview for the position, which she ultimately accepted.

Regardless of how the meeting closes, you will want to follow up, so be sure to keep that opportunity open. If nothing else moves you to close in a friendly manner and follow through accordingly, keep in mind that it's a small world. Make a special point of saying goodbye and thank you to the secretary as you leave.

9
Upon Arrival

Arrive at least half an hour early at the building where your interview will take place. Walk around; check out everything. Giving yourself time to become comfortable in a new environment will help you feel calmer and more confident.

From the moment you walk through the door—in some cases, from the minute you pull into the parking lot—your interview has begun. The person you meet in the lot (or whose space you took because the visitor's lot was full) may turn out to be the one whose support you will need before the final hiring decision is made. The same holds true for whatever might happen at a doorway or in an elevator. You never know when you will be most relieved that you did the right thing.

Reception Room Research

Before you go into the actual interview, there is still time to learn more about the employer, and that knowledge can make the difference in whether you are hired. Arrive at the reception room 10 minutes early. Not only will this give you an opportunity to gain your composure; it will also allow you time to take a close look at the waiting area so you can start to gather the input you will need to decide whether you want to work there. Your arrival in the reception area or at the secretary's desk also means your interview has begun in earnest. The person at that desk may play a bigger role than you might imagine.

In calling on a prospective client, I once walked into a small company's office and introduced myself to the woman who was busy at the first desk I came to. When I asked to speak with Ms. Wilkins, the woman looked up at me, smiled, and said: "I'm the person you're looking for. My secretary's out this afternoon." There was no question that my appointment had already begun.

In many organizations, an executive's secretary frequently has a say in the hire-fire process. In fact, I recall such conversations with some of my own secretaries over the years. A few had been with the employer longer than I, and they had a good sense of who would fit in and who wouldn't.

A secretary can also be the key to whether and how quickly you get to speak with the boss when you make a follow-up call, so treat her as though she has the power she may well have. Take no chances. If nothing else, you at least owe her your thanks for helping to arrange the appointment or for getting you in to see her boss.

Learn the names of the people you meet. That will help increase your comfort level. If you did your homework well, you already know the secretary's name. She is your key to future access to the interviewer. Treat her as you would like to be treated: professionally. If you use her name when you meet her now, you are that much ahead of the game. Everyone enjoys being held in high enough regard to be called by name.

Introduce Yourself

Smile and say who you are, the time of your appointment, and the name of the person with whom you are scheduled to meet. If you don't already know the receptionist's or secretary's name, you might pick it up from a nameplate on the desk. However you learn her name, be sure to use it in your self-introduction. If someone else happens to be sitting at the desk at that moment and you are wrong, no harm is done. You'll get credit for the effort. If you're corrected, accept the correction graciously and use the right name at once. That will be remembered even more.

Pay close attention to the response you receive to your self-introduction. Is it warm and friendly, cool and sterile, cold and unfriendly? Are you offered a seat? A cup of coffee? Are you told your interviewer's status of the moment: "Ms. Ricketson is just finishing up a meeting. Would you mind waiting a few moments and then I'll announce you"? Or does she wave a hand down the hall, snap her chewing gum, and say, "Down there, first door on the right"?

As the organization's first line in greeting newcomers, the receptionist speaks volumes for the organization. If you're later told, "Good help is hard to find," that tells you even more about the firm's perception of itself. The organization's first impressions count too. Learn what you can from them.

Look Around You

While you have the opportunity to do so, look around you. What you will see is the organization's first real statement of how it wishes to identify itself. What should you look for? First examine the decor. French provincial makes a statement different from that of Danish modern. Conservative, perhaps, rather than contemporary? It's worth checking. What pictures are on the walls? Oil portraits of the firm's founding fathers say something far different from, say, glossy studio shots of new products.

What reading material is available? Is there a copy of the annual report? A quarterly report you can browse through? Are copies of trade publications available? Which ones? Skim everything while you wait, especially the most current material on the organization.

One job candidate thumbed through a current issue of an industry-oriented magazine and found an article that said a pending strike could cripple that employer's midwest plant operations. That was a fortunate piece of reading, for the interviewer's first comment, once they were seated, was: "What do you think about that strike possibility at our midwest plant?" Reception room research pays off.

Dealing with Stress

No matter how well you've prepared, it's normal to feel some tension when you first arrive. If you do, use your spare time to walk to the restroom. (Just keep in mind that the interviewer may also be in there.) Step into a booth and stretch, yawn, hang limp at the waist, and bounce up and down. Do whatever you can to help cut your stress load. If you can't get to the restroom and have to remain in view of others, do some discreet breathing and tensing-and-releasing exercises.

Now switch your thoughts away from yourself. Think about what you want to know about the job and the people you would be working with. Envision yourself successfully handling the more difficult questions or situations you might experience. Remind yourself that most executives don't conduct very many interviews and that the person who interviews you may be uneasy. Think about how you might be able to help this individual have a better interview and how your skills might benefit him or her once you're hired.

More Clues If you find time to walk to the restroom, you may pick up additional clues about the organization along the way. What can you notice about the furniture in the offices you pass? What are employees doing? How about the general housekeeping? File the information; it could come in handy later.

Application Forms

You may be given an application form to fill out, even if you are interviewing for a managerial position. Note the way it is given to you and how you are asked to complete it. Again, attitudes will be a measure of what you might expect if you accept employment there. If you thank the individual and say that you will be pleased to clip your résumé to it, what kind of response do you elicit? Are you told, in effect, that either you complete it or you don't get through the door? Are you told this is standard procedure? Are you invited to fill out just the applicant block on the front page and leave the rest blank for now or attach your résumé?

The latter practice is commonly accepted at these levels.

When You're Kept Waiting

It is not unusual for an interviewer to keep a candidate waiting, although the time can vary considerably from appointment to appointment. If you provided the receptionist or secretary with information about yourself, the interviewer may want to take a few minutes to look it over before inviting you in. It is also possible that the interviewer is not task-oriented, can't get it together, is dealing with an unexpected situation that demands attention, or lacks the proper regard for your time.

If the delay is more than 5 minutes beyond the scheduled time and you haven't been given an explanation or apology, inquire. Again the response you receive may tell you more about the organization: "You'll just have to be patient." "I'm sure I don't know." "Oh, this always happens." "I'll see what I can do for you." All send different messages, so be guided accordingly.

If you are told the wait will be more than ten minutes and you receive a reasonable explanation, busy yourself while you remain where you are. If you're told the wait will be longer, ask if there is an empty office you might use to take care of some paperwork and whether the individual might come and get you when the interviewer is ready.

If the delay goes beyond fifteen minutes, or is expected to, you might want to consider offering to reschedule, saying that you "understand how emergencies can crop up." Doing that, however, would not be advisable if you are in another city and would not be able to reschedule the appointment.

10
The Interview Environment

Once you are inside the interviewer's office and the social amenities phase of your meeting is underway, you should have fleeting opportunities to look around the office before you get down to business. Just as you did in the reception area, notice what hangs on the walls, what books are in the bookcase, what personal items are displayed. All these provide clues to the kind of individual you are meeting.

Since many supervisors are not trained as interviewers, your observations may provide you with some needed talking points if the interview stalls. One observant candidate noticed a book on tropical birds among the interviewer's engineering books and asked about it. Until then, the interview had been dying before his eyes.

Relieved, the interviewer perked up; the subject interested him. After a brief conversation in which the candidate asked the interviewer several questions about his interests, the candidate was able to connect with some similar interests and, by using the techniques described later in this book, bridge back into a discussion of the opening. The rest of the interview went well, and two weeks later, the candidate was hired.

Furniture Arrangements

The physical arrangement of offices can be telling. Some people have greater needs for space than others, and some people use space as a way to exercise power or control. Things haven't changed much since Michael Korda wrote about this in *Power*.

Every room in which you might be interviewed has its own dynamics. These are dictated by the way the room is laid out and by other physical aspects such as furnishings.

The indicators are so revealing that you can learn to read a room's power signs with very little practice even when the room is empty. A quick assessment of the interviewer's office can tell you much about the individual and often quite a bit about the department and the organization. In turn, you can use this information to adapt yourself physically and attitudinally to be more comfortable in this new environment.

Since most readers will be interviewed in the offices of managers or executives, let's use an office at that level as our model.

Location Your first indicator of power or status is the location of the office. Is it on an executive floor or on a lower-status floor? Does it occupy a corner or other prestige location or is it one of many similar offices down a corridor? Is it convenient to a restroom, elevators, or a conference room?

Size Is it spacious or cramped? Is it rectangular or corridor style? A corridor style makes it very difficult to arrange furniture in a way that gives the interviewer a sense of space.

Layout Is there more than one door? An office with only one door will enable you to locate the room's "power" area more quickly. When there are two doors, where does each one lead? Does one go to a hallway, or does it go to a private area for the interviewer's secretary? Does the other door open into an area leading to executive offices?

How much space does the interviewer have between the desk and the wall behind him or her? How much space is left for guests? Does the desk face the door so the interviewer can keep his or her eye on it at all times?

Michael Korda, in his book *Power,* described how three common office arrangements create different power dynamics between interviewer and applicant. In the most typical situation, the visitor's chair directly faces the desk of the office's occupant. In this case, the interviewer has the strongest position when his or her desk faces the door but has been pushed away from the back wall. With the extra room behind the desk, the interviewer isn't likely to feel "up against the wall," but the visitor has little breathing room or psychological space, and may feel tightly confined. By contrast, if the desk faces the visitor's chair but is pushed close to the back wall, the applicant has the dominant position. More powerful still for the applicant is a chair that has been placed to one side of the desk. In this situation, the interviewer must turn at an uncomfortable angle to speak with the visitor.

The office may also contain a sofa. If so, you may use that area for social discussion, but move to the desk when it comes time to ask for a decision or a specific action. The sofa area is "semi-social"; the desk area means business.

Lighting Is the office brightly lit, or is the lighting subdued? Is the lighting direct or indirect, fluorescent or incandescent? A high-powered office will have recessed lighting from incandescent bulbs, often in the form of recessed floodlights around the edges of the room.

Housekeeping Is the office tidy? Disorganized? Piled high with projects? Is the interviewer's desk clean? Is the furniture in good condition?

Furnishings Does the interviewer have a desk or a table? How many chairs are there, and what kind are they? Is there a sofa or settee? Are there end tables and a coffee table? Are they made of hardwood or plastic? Are the plants live or artificial? Is the floor carpeted or tiled? Are the wall decorations originals or prints? Are the chairs on castors with swivels or upright? Are they covered with fabric or vinyl?

A high-powered office will have hardwood tables, live plants, carpeting, original artwork, and fabric-covered chairs that roll and swivel. Look for other power symbols such as a high-quality desk set and a second telephone in the informal lounge area of the office.

If you can give yourself a stronger power base in the office, it may be advantageous to do so. For example, you might sit in an upright chair instead of the low, overstuffed one that is offered to you. You might sit with your back to the bright window instead of facing it. You might also move your chair closer to the executive's to take away some of his or her personal space.

Anything that gives you a bit more power may help you in your interview, as long as your moves are not obvious and don't disturb the interviewer.

You can learn much about the interviewer from these assessment techniques. The information is especially important if this individual might become your boss. You will then want to get a better idea of his or her power perceptions and signals.

Group Interviews

In group interviews, you will most likely meet in the interviewer's informal area, if it is large enough, or in a conference room. We'll cover the power dynamics of those situations in a later chapter.

11
The Interviewer's Attitude

First impressions are lasting ones. The employer already has a few ideas of what you may be like just from having looked at the quality and content of the materials you submitted. They must have been acceptable, or you would not have been invited to interview. If you completed an application form while you were waiting for the meeting, that also will be scrutinized. People in the communications fields, particularly advertising, marketing, and public relations, have told me horror stories about prospective employers who sent their letters and résumés back to them without any comment other than the circling of typographical errors.

Before you decide that this may be a clever idea for you to try yourself, however, keep two things in mind: (1) The candidate may not be a good typist or proofreader but may know how to supervise those who have such skills. (2) As we noted earlier, what goes around does indeed come around. No field is so large that one can afford to risk alienating those with whom—or for whom—he or she may one day have to work.

Most people rely on appearance in making their first assessment of others, particularly those who might be working for them one day. As you read earlier, appearance and attire are the most important parts of that first impression. If you have passed the first test, the visual inspection, you should feel comfortable about proceeding to learn more about the interviewer.

Interviewers are people too. They listen on two channels as we all do: They gather facts, but they also gather impressions. How you come across will therefore account for a large portion of the interview's

119

success. The more quickly you get in step, the more smoothly your meeting will flow.

The Handshake

A handshake is always appropriate at the first meeting. Extend your hand and accompany the gesture with a warm, friendly smile. If the other person doesn't respond to the gesture, simply put your hand back down. If there's a problem, it's not yours, nor is it of your making. Of course, people who come across as bonecrushers or limp fish when they shake hands are not well received. If you have wondered what to do about this issue, here is a tip that has worked for many clients:

Look at the interviewer's hand briefly and then at your own, so you know where to connect. Then immediately look at his or her eyes. As you do, think to yourself, "This is an excellent opportunity for both of us." Say, "Thank you for inviting me to meet with you." If you establish the right feelings inside your head, they should travel down through the muscles in the hand, and you will have just the right amount of gripping pressure. Three or four pumps from the elbow should suffice.

Don't complicate your life by using "Pleased to meetcha" or a similar cliché. "Thank you for inviting me to meet with you" works much better. Try it. (And don't be surprised if the *interviewer* responds with a cliché such as: "Oh, it's my pleasure, I'm sure.")

Eye Contact

Much has been written about eye contact. The simplest rule is the best one: Don't shun it, and don't stare. It's important to see each other eye-to-eye, but keep the contact brief, warm, and accepting. Besides helping you to come across well, eye contact will give you a window into the interviewer's thoughts and emotions. You can use it to assess how well you're doing, when to shift gears, when to stop talking, when to amplify a point, and when to ask another question.

Smiles

Yes, there is a *mile* between the two "s" 's, and a warm smile will carry you at least that far emotionally. Science has shown that a smile, even if a little strained at first, actually causes a positive response in the brain. Physiologically, it helps to relieve stress and ease the mind's fight-or-flight concerns.

Voice

Your voice should sound warm and friendly, but not syrupy or condescending. It should convey a certain air of authority and poise, yet it should not come across as aggressive or pompous. It should communicate enthusiasm, yet it should not be boisterous.

If your voice sounds flat, your interviewer may wonder whether you are not in agreement, especially if you responded with flat tones right after you said something with which he or she disagreed strongly. When you speak in a high or nasal voice, your interviewer may feel you are communicating a sense of frustration or lack of control over a situation, as though there were nothing you could do about it.

If you are too loud, the conclusion may be that you are insisting too strongly on making a particular point and possibly that you lack self-confidence in that area. If you begin to mumble or speak too quietly, you may give the impression that you are uncomfortable with your own statement, trying to think out loud, or hoping to fill a nervous pause. If you speak as though you are pushing or pressing, your listener may feel that you are trying to provoke, whether consciously or subconsciously.

To maintain rapport, monitor your own voice tones against the interviewer's. If he or she uses one of these tones momentarily, you can match it briefly, but it is not to your advantage to match a negative tone for long. Instead, shift your own tones toward more congenial ones as quickly as possible.

Personality Types

The interviewers you meet are bound to have different personalities. Although many may try to keep their individual characteristics from showing through, the characteristics are there nonetheless.

The information that follows won't make you an expert in personality analysis, but it should enable you to pick up a few clues that will help you get along better in your interviews. Keep in mind that these are only sorting tools, ways to determine quickly your interviewer's disposition at this particular moment.

Using the four-part personality model discussed in Chapter 1, we saw that everyone has varying elements of the four personality types. Use this information to size up your interviewer's mode at the moment and to gain insight that may guide you in responding effectively.

To employ the technique, you will need to observe the interviewer's word choices, voice tones, and nonverbal signals. As you do, ask yourself:

- Is she trying to approach me or avoid me? If she appears to be using approach behavior, ask yourself whether she is: (1) clearly outgoing, or (2) approachable.
- If you decide she is using avoidance behavior, ask yourself whether she is trying to: (1) keep you away from *her* (pushing you away), or (2) keep herself away from *you* (withdrawing or retreating).

Recognize that you process these impressions through your own personal biases and may be misreading another's signals or calibrating them incorrectly. At best, you are only forming a temporary assessment of the individual's behavior in an effort to establish a better rapport. You may need additional input before you can confirm your first impressions.

Of the four personality types, most interviewers are likely to display, or to try to display, an Approach II side. They want to be perceived as relaxed, in charge, amiable, and receptive to new information. During the interview, they will welcome the interest you show in them and in the job when you tailor your responses and inquiries to the position for which you are interviewing. They are also likely to be receptive when your queries don't make them feel vulnerable. (This might require using such simple threat-reduction techniques as starting a question with "What is it about . . ." rather than "Why on earth. . . .")

As individuals, some interviewers may be more heavily focused on the bottom line (Avoidance I) than others. If you find yourself with an Avoidance I early in your presentation, you should concentrate on the purpose of the interview, as well as on achievements that the interviewer indicates are important.

Your interviewer may seek documentation, acting as an Avoidance II for the moment. Address this need by providing proof and supporting information as you proceed. You should also make an effort to offer reassurances as you summarize. Other interviewers may focus heavily on what people say or have said about you. Approach I people like such testimonials, so let them know who supports your work and what they are saying about it.

Until you determine your interviewer's personality type, it's a good idea to comment in ways that appeal to all four types. This will get you off on the right foot as you continue to gather more input. Keep in mind that the same individual may present an entirely different facet of his or her personality or display a different level of intensity in a later meeting or when the topic changes. Behavior is often circumstantial, so use your initial input only to check whether the interviewer is leaning toward approach or avoidance and active or passive behavior.

Approach Modes

To determine whether an interviewer—let's say a man of about your own age—is in one of the Approach modes, ask yourself these kinds of questions:

- Is he coming on strong? Trying to take over or monopolize the conversation? Being excessively praiseworthy of you or of others?
- Will he yield to you when you indicate a desire to speak? Will he amplify his comments when you ask? Is he selling a personal or organizational agenda? Pushing a favorite point even though it may be irrelevant, or contradictory to what you already know?
- Is he the type who wants honesty at all costs? Is his level of disclosure inappropriate to the circumstances?
- Does he tend to overgeneralize or leave out important details? Is he downplaying a situation that seems serious to you? Is he trying to avoid discussing it further?
- Is he hesitant in expressing personal views? Does he back off quickly after offering a slice of information? Do you sense a deferential attitude?
- Does he appear to be supportive of you? Of others? Of the organization? Of people in general? Is he relaxed and purposeful when commenting?
- Do his overall messages (words, tones, nonverbals) indicate that he is active or passive in his deportment at the moment?

Avoidance Modes

To determine whether your interviewer is displaying avoidance behavior, you should ask yourself:

- What might lie behind the behavior I'm seeing?
- Does he seem offended in some way? Annoyed? (For example, is the timing bad for some reason?)
- Does he have a specific need, say, to impress or persuade you?
- Are there other possibilities?

If you believe that you are facing an Avoidance-mode interviewer—say a middle-aged man—remain calm and try to listen to how this is expressed:

- Does he tend to attack others? If so, is it done by minimizing (damning with faint praise), through ridicule or sarcasm, or by gossiping? Can you find out why?
- Is he trying to compare you unfavorably with others, such as other candidates?
- What exactly is he saying and why is he saying it? Again, can you find out why by asking?
- Is he making demands of you? Are his expectations reasonable? What lies behind them? Are the demands implied or clearly stated?
- Is he trying to control you or the situation? What gives you those impressions? How can you find out what motivates his actions?
- Does his total communication (words, tones, nonverbals) indicate that he is trying to impress you by building himself up? That may appear to be Approach I behavior ("I want you to approach, or like, me.") However, it quickly becomes a turn-off to many, swinging it over to Avoidance I because it pushes you away.

Approach or Avoidance Signals

As you try to determine whether your interviewer is an Approach or Avoidance type, active or passive, postpone all judgmental or defensive thinking. Try not to allow your own feelings to color your opinions. Make mutual understanding your goal. Most interviewers are well-intentioned, and holding that thought in mind may help guide your interview toward a better outcome.

Be sure to check your initial conclusions by asking the questions that will give you concrete feedback. Don't resort to mind reading. Also, avoid the tendency to jump to conclusions. Try to find out what is actually going on or what the interviewer is thinking or trying to do. Carelessness in seeking feedback can lead to false conclusions that don't check out in later discussion.

Who Responds Best to Whom?

Although again, there are no absolutes in this aspect of interviewing, here are some general observations that may contribute to your success.

Approach I individuals tend to respond well to the views or testimonials of others, particularly people whom they recognize as authorities. They tend to like people who present information in a friendly and entertaining way, without a lot of details.

Approach II people are generally the most accepting of the four types. Your challenge will be to encourage them to involve themselves, to encourage their active participation in the interview. You may have to draw them out and defend them against their critics. They prefer specific solutions that contain few risks.

Avoidance I individuals will generally respond best to someone who is well prepared and gets right to the bottom line. They tend to like people who support their points with specific information. They prefer people who agree with their views; they don't take kindly to disagreement; and they will respond best to people who draw them to acceptable conclusions rather than tell them what to do.

Avoidance II people are similar in that they like proof, documentation, and evidence. However, they tend to have more patience than Avoidance I types and generally welcome a discussion of the pros and cons of any important issue. They also like schedules, plans of action, and low-risk situations.

Next we will examine some of the specific ways by which you can build rapport right from the start of your interview.

12
Establishing Rapport

When you interview for a job, body language may have a special significance for you. It can communicate enthusiasm, support, energy, boredom, disagreement, impatience, and much more. Of course, the way a person stands or sits may simply reflect a more comfortable position for him or her at that moment.

We have come a long way from the early studies of body language by such researchers as Ray T. Birdwhistell, who isolated gestures and categorized their presumed meanings. Now most people agree that it is far more effective to consider individuals' nonverbals in clusters, in the context of specific situations.

Nonverbal Messages

It bears repeating: People begin to form impressions of you as soon as you walk through the door for an interview. From the first messages communicated by your appearance and attire, your body language is speaking for you.

ASSIGNING MEANINGS
It's difficult to say what any one gesture or posture may mean when it is isolated from all other signals that the body is capable of sending. Even an obscene gesture can be interpreted in different ways depending on what the eyes, mouth, and particularly body angulation are saying.

Despite what has been written about the meaning of nonverbals, we're not able to pick apart the various signals and come up with

---

SOME STANDARD SIGNALS

In your job interview, you are looking for any clues that will help you determine how well you are coming across. Although circumstances and other signals will determine actual meaning in any situation, here are four overall positions—with commonly accepted interpretations—that are seen frequently in job interviews.

- Arms and legs both crossed: "I'm blocking you." "I'm preoccupied." "I'm not receptive to what you're saying."
- Hand to chin or face: "I'm evaluating what you are saying."
- Lounging with hands folded behind head: "I'm feeling smug; I can top anything you say."
- Open position, with neither arms nor legs crossed: "I'm willing to accept your ideas." If this is done while leaning in toward the speaker, it often indicates even stronger involvement.

---

concrete interpretations, even though certain gestures have taken on specific meanings in our society over the years.

It takes all the body parts to comprise a message, and since the parts are constantly changing, the meanings also are changing. To use body language as a measurement of how your interviewer is receiving you, consider the sum total of signaling body parts such as eyes, mouth, neck, shoulders, back, arms, and legs and overall body posture (standing erect versus slumping or leaning).

You can have a better interview if you observe the interviewer's nonverbals. However, before you can concentrate on nonverbals, you must learn to handle every other aspect of interviewing well enough that you can afford to pay attention to these subtle signals. So be sure you've done your other homework.

OUTWARD EXPRESSIONS

Gestures are considered to be outward expressions of inner emotions, but they can be difficult to interpret. For example, if Joan puts her hand to her head, does this necessarily mean she has made a grooming gesture? She might simply want to scratch an itch.

Does yawning always indicate boredom? No; it could mean a lack of oxygen or an effort to process a conflict between two emotions or thoughts. Sometimes an individual yawns when absorbing new information. Taken out of context, the yawn could be misinterpreted.

Gestures and Postures

Researchers estimate that people can transmit more than 20,000 different gestures by combining their various signaling parts. Gestures in turn can be developed into entire nonverbal "sentences." Unless you devote a career to it, you won't be able to process even a fraction of that number of nonverbal messages. Even trying to pick up on the broad cues can be stressful during a job interview, and sorting the cues into categories may lead to inaccurate readings. If you use the four-part personality model, however, you should be able to achieve greater accuracy and build a better rapport through understanding.

Here are some cues you might pick up as you look at the interviewer's overall posture:

- An Approach I is likely to appear relaxed and lean forward with open posture.
- An Approach II is likely to appear relaxed and sit upright with open posture.
- An Avoidance I is likely to appear tense and lean to one side with closed posture.
- An Avoidance II is likely to appear tense and lean back with closed posture.

A Complex Task

For those who maintain that reading body language is easy, I suggest the following task. (I'm not allowing for the distortions that naturally occur when people receive and process this kind of information through their own filters.) If you care to try it, be sure to do it in environments other than your interviews.

1. Look at people's faces: Do the faces appear angry or hostile? Do they look worried or defensive? Bored or dispassionate? Enthusiastic or eager? Active or involved? Supportive or understanding? Calm or complacent? Curious or puzzled? Do you see any other emotions? Check this out through courteous questioning.

2. Notice the tilt of the individual's head. Because the head is so prominent a part of the body, many people notice it early on. Is the individual's head tilted up? Down? Forward? Back? To the side? Held symmetrically and balanced? Check your observations in the same way.

Consider what it would be like to do the same thing with all the other signaling parts of the body. Perhaps you are ready to agree that it might be enough for now to be able to assess who's with you and who isn't. If so, let's continue on with the task at hand and keep to a discussion of this interesting topic in perspective.

Your Interviewer's Other Language

As you saw toward the end of Chapter 6, people tend to rely on words having to do with their visual, auditory, and tactile senses—their representational systems—to translate and process information about life around them. How an individual does that, and which system he or she uses, may change with circumstances. People tend to prefer one mode in a particular situation or at any given moment. So be sure to monitor their messages for word choices as well as content. Match the mode an interviewer is using, and you will facilitate communication because you will be transmitting through the same channel. Practice doing this before you schedule an interview and in your interview rehearsals.

A researcher named Edgar Dale developed what is now known as "Dale's Cone of Experience." According to Dale, people generally remember 20 percent of what they hear, 30 percent of what they see, 50 percent of what they hear and see, and 80 percent of what they hear, see, and do. So, to make the most solid impression possible, build from the interviewer's primary mode and engage the other two modes whenever opportunities present themselves.

Gaining Rapport Skills

You can establish a further rapport with your interviewer if you monitor the rate of speech and match that as well. Speech rate also tells you about the individual's mode: A person who speaks rapidly is generally processing information in the visual mode. One who speaks at a moderate rate is usually in auditory. A person who speaks slowly is most likely in a tactile mode.

As you saw in the preceding chapter, you can also match a person's voice tones, pitch, intensity, and inflections. Just be careful to sound sincere, not as though you are mocking. Be particularly sensitive in this respect when it comes to matching an accent or regional dialect.

It will take a bit of extra effort to attend to this additional information and still keep track of the content of what the interviewer is saying. It is worth the effort because the interviewer's impressions of you will be built upon your ability to establish an early rapport.

WHAT PEOPLE REMEMBER

Widely accepted figures indicate that your interviewer will forget up to 40 percent of what you've said after only 20 minutes, 60 percent after half a day, and 90 percent after a week. Furthermore, a well-known study by Albert T. Mehrabian shows that, of any communication, approximately 55 percent is transmitted through body language, 38 percent through voice tones, and only 7 percent through actual content. When it comes to *what* you say, most people can generally recall no more than nine "bits" of information, at best, shortly after they hear them. (Researchers refer to this as Miller's Law of Seven, plus or minus two.) So the other message here is to keep your content sharply focused and your explanations simple.

ADDITIONAL TOOLS FOR RAPPORT

You will help your interviewer follow along best when you:

- Proceed from areas of agreement to areas of uncertainty, from the known to the unknown. You can enhance the likelihood of acceptance if you build strong bridges or transitions between any two such sets.
- Clarify your own career goals in your meeting; discuss the steps that would have to be taken in the hiring process; review the goals and objectives that go with the position; and ask the interviewer how he or she would know when a candidate is the right one.
- Put yourself into the position as often as you can without becoming overbearing. For example, "That's interesting, Alison. If I were in the position, how would that actually work?" Follow up the reply by saying that, assuming you were hired for the position, you believe the plan outlined would work well.
- Relate everything you say to the question at hand and to the position being discussed.
- Invite the interviewer to become actively involved in a mock scenario and then be sure you participate actively. "Let's see now, Alison. If we were actually doing that, how would it go?"
- Do your best to keep the environment mutually supportive.

What You See

Whatever behavior you observe is simply that: behavior you observe. Since we are all in charge—or at least try to be in charge—of our emotions, behavior reflects the way the interviewer has chosen to be. Try to see attitudes for what they are, and see what you can do to understand them and to help the individual be more successful. Then you are less likely to be intimidated.

What's at Stake for the Interviewer

Here are some other attitudinal observations you might want to keep in mind as your interview progresses:

Professional On a professional level, the interviewer needs to make the right decision and be perceived as having good judgment. Therefore, you should ask yourself whether the interviewer is thinking and talking about the good of the organization as a whole. If so, your comments should address that. Ask questions about the organization and use the interviewer's replies to show how you would be a good fit.

Personal Person-to-person, it is logical for most interviewers to want to be liked and accepted. Here, too, you can show how you would fit in, this time as a coworker and an employee the interviewer would want to have on staff. The "we" approach is a good one here. For example, when the interviewer describes a challenging task, it might be appropriate to ask: "How would we ordinarily deal with a situation like that?"

Other Assurances Your questions and comments should also show that you recognize and respect your interviewer's level of responsibility and capability. They should also convey an appropriate amount of respect for authority, letting the interviewer feel knowledgeable and in charge.

Moving On

You have done everything you can to deal with personal, content, and environmental considerations. You have gone through the social amenities portion of the interview. You are about to get down to business.

Be sure you put yourself in a posture that exudes confidence, and remain alert to what happens next. Show the interviewer a friendly face. Sit toward the front edge of your chair, and lean slightly toward the interviewer.

You may cross your legs at the ankles or position one foot slightly in front of the other, but don't cross your legs at the knee. That creates a physical stress point, inhibits deep breathing, and causes tension.

Position your hands lightly on your lap with your palms facing inward. Don't be tempted to grasp the arms of the chair. That posture may look great for Lincoln's statue, but in an interview, it could make you look as though you're in the electric chair.

As you speak, allow yourself to gesture immediately. The more quickly you get your hands moving under your control, the more quickly you will burn off any residual stress, lubricate your voice, and increase your feelings of confidence.

Now it's time to find out what kind of interview your potential employer is conducting.

13
The Four Types of Interviews

Let's review the purpose of the employment interview so we can analyze what comes next. The employment interview is an opportunity to exchange information and determine whether your skills and the employer's job opening are a good match. If you keep that in mind once you're into the interview, you should have no difficulty with whatever type of interview confronts you.

Interview Formats

Interview formats differ with the style of the person who conducts them. To understand their style, it will help to know about the four interview formats that job candidates experience most often: stress, open-ended, narrative, and standard Q&A.

THE STRESS FORMAT
Suppose your interview starts out something like this: "Your résumé isn't particularly impressive. So tell me why I should hire you." Clearly, your host—let's say a man in his thirties—is conducting a stress interview. He may be quite skilled and doing this intentionally. If the position is highly stressful, he has probably decided to structure the meeting in this way to find a candidate who can take the heat. The key to responding is simple: Attitude is everything, content is secondary. Your reply might go something like this.

Take a deep but not obvious breath. Pause, smile slightly—if only to show that you now know the game—and, in an evenly modulated voice, say, "You seem to be trying to see how I handle stressful situations. Is that a fair guess?" Then remain silent until you receive an answer.

Notice that you said "seem to" and followed up your statement with a question designed to have the interviewer deny or verify your appraisal or clarify his intention. He might have one of three responses:

1. Total silence coupled with staring, designed to cause you to blurt out another response. Simply respond in kind, with silence. The game is on. If no one speaks after a given period of time, you can thank the interviewer for his time, let him know you might consider participating in a more productive interview at another time, and leave. The interviewer will either break off the gambit or let you go. If it's the latter, you may be glad you left.

However, the interviewer may choose instead to break the silence with a badgering reply, such as, "What's the matter? Can't you just answer the question?" If this happens, ask the interviewer to repeat the question. On the second go-round, it usually loses some steam. Your reply at that point might go like this: "If I understand correctly, what you're asking is whether my qualifications meet the requirements. Perhaps you'd like to tell me more about the position. Apparently there is reason for me to want to know more."

2. Instead of responding to your initial query with silence, the interviewer may try to poke holes in some of the information presented in your résumé. It might go like this: "Why, just look here. It says you directed an inventory computerization. I suppose you're going to tell me you did that all by yourself."

Your reply (still remaining in control): "On the contrary, several people participated in that project. It was a tough one, and it took a real team effort to get it done. Is it the kind of project that I would be doing in the job we are talking about?"

At this point, he may choose to drop the challenging approach and get down to a more fruitful discussion. You may still want to keep your guard up a little, however. Stay in charge of your attitude and emotions. No one can do anything to you that you are not willing to have done. If the tactics continue and you begin to feel too intimidated, you can simply say so, excuse yourself from the interview, and leave. Again, you probably wouldn't want to work there anyhow.

3. Finally, the interviewer might give up the gambit right away upon hearing you handle your initial response to the stress question so well.

He may explain why it seemed necessary to test you in that way, and then proceed to tell you more about the position. At that point, the interview may switch to one of the other formats.

If the interviewer opens with stressful questions but is a rank amateur, you can probably break up the game quickly and get down to business. He may not have realized the impact of the question, or he may have been trying to be clever. Your professionalism will channel things in a better direction.

There are, of course, other ways in which an interview can be stressful. Stress can result from such environmental elements as uncomfortable seating, bright lights, and noise. It can be brought about by disruptions or even by erratic pacing. Sometimes interview stress is created through the selection of open-ended questions designed to embarrass the candidate or create uneasiness.

THE OPEN-ENDED FORMAT

If the interviewer, again our man in his thirties, opens with something like, "Well now, tell me all about yourself," he has begun what may be an open-ended interview. If this is the case, you will be asked questions that you could respond to in many ways. The interviewer, if skilled, may monitor your responses closely to assess your priorities, sense of direction, and ability to focus on the issue at hand, among other things. Just stay alert to the task, keep your answers brief, and keep relating them to how your skills fit the available opening.

An unskilled interviewer who uses this approach may simply not feel like talking. In fact, he may have already written you off and may be going through the interview only to fulfill an obligation. It will be your job to engage the interviewer in the process if you hope to succeed.

Many open-ended interviews contain early questions that would be difficult for the candidate to answer without having further input. For example, you might be asked to describe why you believe you are qualified for the opening. If no one has described the job to you, you can't do this very well. Don't guess; ask. If you need more information in order to respond appropriately, say so—no matter what the question might be.

THE NARRATIVE FORMAT

You would think that not too many interviewers would open with a narrative type of interview, but a surprising number of candidates have said that it is more common than we might imagine. "I can remember when I was about your age, looking to move to the big city, just as you are. It seems like only yesterday. In fact, during the twenty years that I've been here. . . ."

Such an interviewer, say a woman in her sixties, may be acting out of nervousness or egocentricity, depending upon what she chooses to ramble on about. However, the technique could also indicate a person who wants to monitor your nonverbal responses or your skill at handling the situation. Finally, it may be an effort toward "full disclosure," a desire to give you all the facts.

How do you handle this one? Let her ramble a bit, but any time you think you've heard the end of a sentence, use whatever you can from the monologue to ask a question that will bring the discussion back to the job. The interviewer may go on again for a while, but at least what you hear should be more relevant. You can ask questions that show your knowledge of the organization. You can also ask the interviewer to tell you more about the job itself. In any case, you may need to work to get the information you must have to make a sound decision. The interviewer's style may be a sufficient tip-off if she will be your boss.

THE STANDARD Q&A FORMAT

Finally, we come to the interviewer, let's say a brisk young woman, who seems determined to make your interview a productive experience for both of you. This interview might open with a stage setter and a first question that might go like this:

"This morning, I would like to cover the following areas of discussion with you: the job that is open, the department itself, and the company and its role. Then I'd like you to discuss your background and experience as they might relate to the opening. Let's both feel free to raise questions at any time. Now, about the job. . . ."

This is your standard Q&A interview, and it is the most productive and most frequently used of all. In the next chapter we will discuss the areas of questioning you might be expected to address during your interview.

14
What You Will Be Asked

You now know about the types of interviews you might experience, so let's consider the areas of questioning you might expect. Regardless of the questions that you might be asked, the bottom line for most interviews is to provide the interviewer with input in three areas. Let's examine them one at a time and see how the interviewer might elicit information in each area. In Chapters 16 and 17, we'll cover techniques and strategies you can use in responding to the questions in each of the three areas.

Your Factual Background

Interviewers can obtain factual information about you through simple, direct questions. They must avoid asking questions that would put them in violation of the law. However, some interviewers may not be aware of what the law allows or does not allow, and that can pose some difficult choices for the candidate. We'll cover illegal questions in detail in Chapter 18.

Your Opinions and Viewpoints

Interviewers will also want to know your positions on various issues, particularly those that may affect their organizations. Although your responses in those areas may have little bearing on what you will do on the job, the interviewer will be hoping to learn more about how you might deal with issues once you're hired. Regrettably, few line executives who interview are so well trained that they can interpret your answers effectively to see how the views you express might apply to issues in a broader sense.

Typical questions in this area might have to do with your belief systems. They could include:

"Legislation that would affect your field of employment has been proposed. What do you think of it?"

"What about ethics in business really turns you off?"

"Where do you stand on the issue of foreign competition?"

Your Temperament or Personality

In this area, interviewers will seek to find out where you fit in. They may want to know whether you are oriented more toward Approach, meaning that you prefer to work with people, or more toward Avoidance, meaning that you prefer to work alone.

Numerous lists of personality types are used to describe managers, but these types seem to come up most frequently: analyzer, balancer, blamer, boss, catalyst, computer, collector, compiler, compromiser, destroyer, detailer, director, distracter, dominator, facilitator, influencer, justifier, leveler, overseer, placater, planner, relater, socializer, stabilizer, and thinker.

The labels are self-explanatory, but they are simply that: labels. In an employment interview, the potential employer may want to put you on a particular shelf. Everyone likes to know where things, including people, fit into his or her life.

However, this kind of labeling in particular is distortive and fails to take into account what the candidate might be like in less stressful situations: how he or she might come across on the job.

If employers want to gain input that can help them make quick, tentative assessments as interviews proceed, they might consider the four personality types described in Chapter 1. These types can provide handy reference points for ongoing evaluations.

It is important to keep in mind, however, that sorting by personality types does not mean pigeonholing. It will best serve an interviewer who is willing (and has the skills) to continue to monitor and check observations as the interview progresses. Few interviewers may be able to do that.

Still other interviewers may attempt to sort their candidates more specifically by traits, labels that would tell them more about the applicant's temperament. Lists of such traits, and methods for arriving at them, are endless. Once again, however, one would have to question the average interviewer's skill and qualifications for conducting such test-ing—even through an interview.

Nonetheless, the people who interview you will want to know what makes you tick, what you might be like on the job. They will gather this information in the best way they know how: through their own personal filters, which may not provide accurate readings.

The solution, if there is one? Just be the best *you* that you know how to be. Don't try to second-guess, and don't try to pretend to be some-thing you're not. In the long run, your honesty will take you through the door into the position that is right for you.

Down to Specifics

Sooner or later, the business aspect of every interview comes down to this: the questions you are likely to be asked and how you will answer them. If you regard all questions as opportunities, you'll be most likely to have a successful interview no matter what subjects are raised and no matter how the questions are phrased.

Since the legality of a given question may depend on varying state laws, who is asking the question, why the information may be needed, and the way the question is phrased, I have included "questionable" questions so they don't come as a surprise later on.

You certainly won't be asked all the following questions during an employment interview, but you might hear many of them over several such meetings. For your convenience, I have grouped them by category, but a few may not seem to fit perfectly. Practice them at home.

About the Company

- Why would you want to work for us?
- What do you know about our company?
- How do your skills fit this job opening?
- Do any of your friends or relatives work here?
- Have you ever handled money or confidential information?
- Have you ever been bonded?

About Your Knowledge of the Company

- What do you know about our company and where it stands within our particular field?

- How would our company gain by hiring you?
- Based on your knowledge of the field, who would you say are our major competitors?
- What position would you like to hold ten years from now?
- Why would you like to work for our company?
- Have you ever worked for this company under another name?
- How would you define your long-range goals and objectives?

Relating Your Background to the Opening

- How does your experience qualify you for this job?
- If you are presently working, why would you want to change jobs at this time?
- Here is a problem related to your area of specialty. What could you contribute to its resolution?

About the Job Itself

- Are you willing and able to work overtime? Under what circumstances?
- How do you feel about relocating?
- Are you willing to take a lie detector test as a condition of being hired?
- Would you have any interest in working flex-time, part-time, or some schedule other than a regular work week?
- We require medical examinations as a condition of employment. Are you willing to have such an examination by a doctor we select?
- If hired, when would you be able to start working?
- Would you have any problems commuting, getting in on time, working a full day, or maintaining good attendance?
- How long would you plan to stay with our company?

About Your Abilities

- Why did you choose this field?
- What special job-related skills do you have?
- What personal and professional traits do you feel are essential for success in your field?

About Previous or Current Employment

- How did your previous employer treat you?
- How did you secure your previous job?
- Were you ever dismissed from a job? For what reason?

- How do you happen to be unemployed at the moment?
- Does your employer know you are looking for another job?
- What type of work do you do best or enjoy most and least?
- Which of your former employers did you like best and why?
- Why are you no longer there?
- You seem to have held the same job for a long time without a promotion. What can you tell me about that?
- Would a lack of advancement opportunities cause you to look elsewhere?
- Have you ever been fired or asked to resign? Explain.
- Can you explain the gaps in your employment history?
- Why have you held so many jobs in such a short period of time?

About Salary

- What kind of money are you looking for?
- What was your most recent salary?
- Would you ever work without pay? Under what circumstances?
- What supplementary income do you have?
- What was your salary progression in your last job?
- Why are you not making more money at this stage in your life?
- What were your starting and highest salaries on your previous job?
- What salary do you expect with us?
- How important to you is salary in deciding to take a job?

About Your Finances

- Do you own life insurance, a car, or a home?
- Describe your financial status and obligations at this time.
- Did you contribute toward your family's finances or your own education?
- Have you maintained a regular savings program?
- How good are you at budgeting?
- What are your outstanding debts right now?

About Your Academic Preparation

- Why did you select your major?
- Which courses did you like and dislike most?
- What was the most difficult subject and why?
- What was your grade point average in high school and college?
- Are you enrolled in any programs for self-improvement or college credit, or do you plan to enroll in any?

- Have you ever dropped out of a course or out of school?
- What was your major in college, and what minor subjects did you take?
- What courses did you find most exciting and beneficial?
- What courses did you feel were boring or a waste of time?

About Your Outside Interests

- How do you spend your spare time?
- How do you spend vacations?
- Of which clubs and organizations are you a member?
- What offices have you held in outside organizations?
- Are such activities worth your time? How much time?
- Describe other outside activities that will demonstrate your leadership skills.
- What do you do to keep in good physical health?
- What do you do for relaxation?

About Your Job-Related Personality

- What was your last boss like?
- What is your style of working?
- What do you want most out of a job?
- How did your previous employer treat you? Please explain.
- What do you know about our firm's management style?
- Where would you like to be after five years? After ten years?
- Are you more comfortable working alone or in large groups?
- If your supervisor were unfair to you or difficult to work with, how would you handle it?
- How well organized are you?
- Do you work better as a member of a team or independently?
- Are you willing to take calculated risks when necessary?
- Would you fire incompetent workers, or keep them but reduce your demands on them if they needed the jobs?
- What personal attributes make for the best supervisor?
- What would your present (or most recent) employer criticize about your work? Be specific.
- What personal sacrifices would you be prepared to make to succeed on the job?
- What is the worst thing that has happened to you in a job? What is the best?

- Do you have mixed emotions about working for a person considerably younger than you are or who makes more money than this position pays?
- What are your major professional strengths? How have you capitalized on them?
- What do you consider to be your major weaknesses? How have they affected you on the job?
- Describe the most difficult work assignment you ever tackled. How did it turn out?
- As a supervisor, what procedure would you follow in recommending the dismissal of a worker who has proved to be inadequate on the job?
- How important do you feel it is to be well-connected?
- What suggestions have you made in previous jobs that helped the organizations?
- What suggestions were turned down, and how do you feel about the outcome?

About Your General Personality

- Tell me about yourself.
- What are your major strengths? Weaknesses?
- What kind of people do you like? Dislike?
- What was your home life like when you were a child?
- How good is your memory for names and faces?
- What four or five words would best describe you? Why?
- Do you consider yourself a leader or a follower?
- What do people think of you? In your opinion, are they right?
- How do you cope under pressure?
- How do you handle criticism?
- How do you react when things don't go your way?
- Do you have any mental or emotional conditions that might interfere with your performance on the job?
- How do you feel about doing detail work?
- Tell me how you handle routine work.
- Describe your problem-solving abilities.
- What do you believe it takes to succeed in business?
- Are you comfortable with making decisions, even difficult ones? Describe.
- If we offered you this job, would you make the decision whether to accept it on your own, or in consultation with others? Describe who.
- What type of people attract you? What kind do you shy away from?

- What rubs you the wrong way?
- Succinctly, tell me the story of your life, highlighting the aspects that made you what you are today.
- Who would you say has had the greatest influence on your life?
- What attributes do you look for in a friend?
- What does it take to make you happy?
- Can you tell me something about your family?
- Are you generally inclined to hold center stage in a group or organization?

About Personal Matters

- How do you spend your vacations and spare time?
- In what ways are you active in community work and social, fraternal, civic, or other organizations?
- What professional associations or trade journals help keep you abreast of developments in your field?
- You indicated that you are divorced. Would you like to tell me how this might be a factor in your job performance?
- When was your last physical checkup?
- Are you under a doctor's care? For what reason?
- Over the past year, how much time have you lost from work and for what reason?
- If you are not a U.S. citizen, do you have the legal right to work in this country?
- Have you ever violated the law, aside from such minor offenses as traffic violations, speeding, and illegal parking?
- Have you ever been convicted of a major offense? If so, explain.
- Do you take narcotics or other drugs with or without a prescription?
- Have you served in the armed forces? If so, in what branch and what was your rank? What is your present military status?
- Do you have a driver's license? Has it ever been revoked? Describe.

General

- Are you considering other job offers at the moment? If so, which ones?
- On what basis will you make your decision?
- What references may we check at this time?
- What questions do you have?

How Questions Are Asked

Frequently the way a question is asked can have more impact than the actual content of the question on a candidate's ability to respond. Keeping in mind that there are no bad questions, only the possibility of giving bad answers, here are the types of questions that commonly occur in all kinds of interviews, including those for screening prospective employees.

WORST-LEAST QUESTIONS
Be especially wary of questions that ask you to address most-least or best-worst aspects of the issue raised: for example, "What kinds of people do you like most (least)?" You can reply best to such questions with moderate responses on both sides. You might want to lean somewhat toward the positive side so you don't appear too extreme or too far outside the interviewer's way of thinking. You can deal with the negative side by coming up with good negatives—statements that include something the interviewer would agree is a positive in disguise. For example, you might want to say that the people you like least are those who are unfair to others.

DIFFICULT QUESTIONS
In any interview, you are bound to be asked questions at least as difficult as those listed in this chapter. Whenever you receive such questions, always try to isolate the point of the question and make sure your reply is somehow relevant to the position for which you are being interviewed.

Most of the questions you receive will not be intentionally difficult. In fact, many will be efforts to clarify or understand information you have already provided. That is why attitude is so important.

ATTITUDE
During every minute of your interview, hold fast to the attitude that you and the interviewer are there to help one another. Assume that the interviewer will be friendly unless you alienate him or her. Find areas of agreement or commonality whenever possible.

In discussing the fight-or-flight reaction to stress, I noted that neither fighting nor leaving would keep you in the running for a job opening. No matter what happens, stay in charge of your own pace and remain calm. Strive for understanding. Bad attitude is a frequent reason for not hiring an individual; an interviewer who finds that you can easily be aroused or perturbed is likely to wonder how you might handle more stressful situations on the job. Regard each question as an opportunity to show how courteous and cooperative you can be.

Questioning Techniques

Since you have prepared yourself well for your interview, you should be able to provide relevant and informative responses to any questions. However, television has taught people how to ask questions in more sophisticated ways, creating new challenges for any job candidate. In many cases, the techniques for asking questions have outstripped the techniques for responding to them well. Understanding the techniques will help you even further. To help restore the balance, then, here are the techniques you are most likely to experience:

Technique: Needling
Example: "Do you really believe I'll buy that?"
Response: Stick by your guns; don't equivocate or vacillate. Say, "Absolutely, Diane." Then go on to support your position.

Technique: Errors of fact
Example: "So you made a quarter million on that contract?"
Response: If necessary, correct the number graciously and then go on to show its relevancy to the opening.

Technique: Reinterpretation of your response
Example: "So what you're saying is that you wouldn't be willing to work overtime."
Response: Clarify your position.

Technique: Putting words in your mouth
Example: "So you'd say such people are tyrants."
Response: Use only the words with which you are comfortable.

Technique: False assumption or conclusion
Example: "So if you don't like something, you could walk off the job."
Response: In your response, don't agree with the assumption, but clarify what your position would be.

Technique: Hypothetical question
Example: "If we were unable to provide a stock plan to your liking, you probably wouldn't accept the job."

Response: Acknowledge the hypothetical nature of the question and then encourage the interviewer to discuss what actually might be available.

Technique: Baiting you into accusations
Example: "What do you really think of your former boss?"
Response: Don't get caught in the trap. Say nothing negative about anyone.

Technique: Leading question
Example: "If we can't come up with a fixed-schedule review program for you, what would your next step be?"
Response: As with speculative and hypothetical questions, don't be led down a path you do not choose to take.

Technique: Multiple-part
Example: "When you were in college, how were your grades? Were you involved in any sports? Any extracurricular activities? Did you hold any offices?"
Response: Pick the part you *want* to answer and reply to that. You are under no obligation to try to remember and respond to every part.

Technique: Forced choice
Example: "Which would you rather have, a boss who is never around or one who is constantly on your back?"
Response: Watch the loaded words here; then make your *own* selection. Choose either part, both parts, or neither part of these options.

Again, keep in mind that you are in charge of you. Since the interviewer's impression of you counts more than the content of your answers, how you respond becomes more important than what you say. The next chapter will address some of the skills you will need if you are to make certain that your responses are well considered. Also, I will show you how to ask questions of your own to get the information you need to decide whether this job is right for you.

15
It's Your Turn

Any good employment interview consists of a dialogue rather than periods in which one party plays the role of inquisitor and the other merely responds. If the session takes on an aura of prosecuting attorney versus defendant, the interviewer either is unskilled or is attempting to conduct a stress interview.

If an interview is to serve your needs as well as the interviewer's, it should be conversational, meaning roles should be exchanged whenever doing so will contribute to mutual understanding.

Not only do you have a right to ask questions whenever they occur to you, you also have an actual obligation to yourself to do so. Later in this chapter, we'll examine some of the questions from Chapter 14 in detail and discuss the reasons why you may want—and need—to respond with questions of your own before you attempt to answer the interviewer's question. Your goal will be to ensure that you are answering the right question in the right way. It's much like the mother who launched into a discussion of the facts of life when her 5-year-old asked where he came from, only to find out afterward that the child merely wanted to know the name of the hospital in which he was born.

Throughout each interview, the opportunities to ask questions will become evident to you. You need not wait until the interview ends to try to squeeze in the questions you need answered. However, no matter whether or not the opportunities are evident, there are certain questions that you will need answered in order to make an appropriate decision.

Your Questions

Review the questions that follow and develop a list that will help you get the information you need. Don't hesitate to type the most important questions on an index card and take the card to the interview with you.

About the Job

- Is this position permanent or temporary?
- Why is it vacant?
- How long has it been vacant?
- May I speak with the person who held it previously?
- Do you have a job description I might see for this opening?
- To whom would I report?
- Would it be feasible for me to look around the department?
- Might I talk with a few of the people with whom I would be working?
- What aspect of this job is hardest to find a candidate for?
- How many people would report to me?
- How long has each person who would report to me been on the job?
- How much would I be expected to travel?
- What would you say the firm's major assets and liabilities are?

About the Future

- How long did the former occupant hold this job?
- How does the salary range compare with that of other members of the department?
- Please describe your salary and advancements program.
- Would a relocation be likely at any time?
- What is the company's policy concerning promotion from within?
- How are salary increases determined: merit, testing, length of service, or some other means?
- How will you know when you have found the perfect candidate?
- How soon after the interview will I know whether I am hired?

About Your Personal Needs and Interests

- Please tell me the company's policy on benefits, pension plans, salary increases, promotions, hospitalization and insurance, stock sharing, company car, and memberships in trade or professional associations or unions. (Don't ask this all at once.)

As you probably began to realize as you read through this list, some of the questions you will need answered probably do not appear on the list, but hopefully you have been inspired by it. Develop your own list, and have it ready.

Probes and Verbal Redirects

Let's consider the questions you may want to ask before you even attempt to answer questions similar to "Mommy, where did I come from?"—the kind that can lead you down the wrong path unless you are prepared.

You have every right to probe such questions, and a responsible interviewer will answer them for you rather than press you to attempt a reply. Again, attitude is everything, so respond to each vague or open-ended question with something such as this:

"I can understand that you would need that information, so could you help me by clarifying . . . ?"

"Let me try to respond to that for you. Would you like me to focus on how my work might be affected by what you're asking, or something else?"

"There are many ways one might reply to that: Would you mind telling me how you would like me to respond?"

"It would be hard to come up with an appropriate answer without knowing more about the specific situation you have in mind. Could you tell me about it?"

These are just a sampling. Review the questions in Chapter 14 to see how many of them you might respond to with probe questions of your own. We'll consider some typical ones here to help you through this process.

When you do respond, however, keep in mind that you are under no obligation to go down a path that is not of your own choosing. You can redirect a response toward an area that is more relevant to the task at hand.

For example, when you are asked something of a personal nature that seems irrelevant to the job, you might open with a probe question, listen carefully to the direction the interviewer wants you to take, address that area in general terms, and then branch off into something more relevant.

Let's say the interviewer is talking about appropriate attire on the job and suddenly asks: "What do you think about the skirt lengths coming into style this fall?" Your probe might be: "Perhaps I'm missing something here. How might that relate to this position?" If the interviewer responds with something such as: "Well, after all, we have a professional image to uphold," you might want to probe further by asking whether skirt length has something to do with professionalism and if so, how. Or you might go immediately to a verbal redirect and say something like this: "I agree. Professionalism is very important on the job. I'm sure you'll find [future pacing] that my wardrobe reflects the appropriate standards."

Sample Questions and Probe Responses

AREA: *Your Opinions and Viewpoints*
QUESTION: "The proposed legislation on recycling would affect your field of employment. What do you think of it?"
YOUR PROBE RESPONSE: "I'm sure that legislation will be important to everyone. It would be interesting to know how Myers and Whitney feels about it."

AREA: *Your Temperament or Personality*
QUESTION: "How do you feel about people who pass the buck?"
YOUR PROBE RESPONSE: "That makes me wonder if you are referring to an actual situation here. If it's something I would be expected to deal with, could you be a little more specific so that I have enough input to answer the question more effectively?"

AREA: *The Company*
QUESTION: "How do your skills fit this job opening?"
YOUR PROBE RESPONSE: "It would be difficult for me to respond to that specifically until I know more about the job. Can we go into that now?"

AREA: *Your Knowledge of the Company*
QUESTION: "Why would you like to work for our company?"
YOUR PROBE RESPONSE: "I've looked into that, and I have a number of good reasons. But I would like to know more about this *department's* mission. Could you develop that so we can see how my reasons fit?

AREA: *Your Background as Related to the Opening*
QUESTION: "Why do you want to change jobs?"

YOUR PROBE RESPONSE: "I'm not entirely sure I want to. That depends on finding a place where I can make more use of my computer specialties. Would that be possible here?"

AREA: *The Job Itself*
QUESTION: "How do you feel about relocating?"
YOUR PROBE RESPONSE: "I certainly don't rule it out. Is it relevant to this job?" (If it is, you will want to know where, when, and so on before you respond.)

AREA: *Your Abilities*
QUESTION: "What personal and professional traits do you consider essential to success in your field?"
YOUR PROBE RESPONSE: "I think the skills I've developed have been very important to my success so far. Where I go from here will depend on my employer's needs and the opportunities that become available. Could you shed some light on those points?"

AREA: *Previous or Current Employment*
QUESTION: "Would the lack of advancement opportunities cause you to look elsewhere?"
YOUR PROBE RESPONSE: "That depends. Could you elaborate a bit for me? Do you perceive this to be a dead-end job?"

AREA: *Salary*
QUESTION: "What kind of money are you looking for?"
YOUR PROBE RESPONSE: "That depends. There might be good reasons to start at less than I make now—opportunity for advancement, for example. And there are some jobs for which I feel a higher salary would be appropriate—perhaps to put me on a par with people I would be supervising. What can you tell me about the salary range offered here?"

AREA: *Your Finances*
QUESTION: "Describe your financial status and obligations at this time."
YOUR PROBE RESPONSE: "I'm sure you must have a good reason for asking that. Would you mind telling me what's behind your question so that I might consider an appropriate response?" (Your response

could also be to respectfully decline to answer this personal question.)

AREA: *Academic Preparation*

QUESTION: "Are you enrolled in any programs for self-improvement or college credit, or do you plan to enroll in any?"

YOUR PROBE RESPONSE: "Not at present. But I would be interested in knowing the company's position on that. Could you fill me in?"

AREA: *Outside Interests*

QUESTION: "Do you feel that professional organizations are worth your time? How much time?"

YOUR PROBE RESPONSE: "They certainly can be worthwhile, depending on the circumstances. What is Myers and Whitney's policy on that?"

AREA: *Your Job-Related Personality*

QUESTION: "What do you know about our firm's management style?"

YOUR PROBE RESPONSE: "It's difficult to really know much about it from the outside. Obviously, it's been successful. Perhaps that's something you can tell me about. I'd appreciate knowing your own perceptions."

AREA: *Your General Personality*

QUESTION: "What type of people attract you? What kind do you shy away from?"

YOUR PROBE RESPONSE: "I find I can get along with just about anyone by respecting individual differences. What kind of people might I be working with here?"

AREA: *Personal Matters*

QUESTION: "What professional associations or trade journals help keep you abreast of developments in your field?"

YOUR PROBE RESPONSE: "I belong to the Boston Computer Society and subscribe to *PC World* and *PC Magazine.* I'd add to that if it would help me here. Which ones do you feel might be most important?"

AREA: *General*

QUESTION: "If you are offered this job, on what basis will you make your decision?"

YOUR PROBE RESPONSE: "I'd have to have more information. Can you tell me more about the opening here?"

A General Rule

There are no guarantees that the probe technique will work in every situation in which you feel you need more information before you respond. It will, however, help keep this general rule in mind: *Find out everything you need to know about the question and the interviewer's intention in asking it before you commit yourself to an answer. Don't hang yourself by answering too quickly or inappropriately. You have a right to receive the input you need before you reply. Caution: Use this technique sparingly—only when you need it. Overuse could turn your interviewer off.*

16
Dealing with Questioners and Disagreements

Since few interviewers have negative intentions, it will help you to know more about the good as well as the bad and to examine the roles interviewers play when they ask their questions. The roles may be as brief as the questions themselves. However, they are valid and should help you understand the interviewing process even better.

Supporters They agree with what you are saying and tend to lead you into areas that will showcase your skills. Accept this support graciously and build upon it in your responses. Just don't become boastful.

Detailers Give these people as many facts as they are willing to collect. Respond to their questions with the specifics they are seeking.

Filibusterers You'll find them running narrative interviews. Regrettably, you can't be clever in turning them off. Just wait them out and ask questions that, by their nature, showcase the fact that you are prepared for the interview and qualified to do the job.

Wanderers and Drifters If the question is too far off the subject, gently bring the questioner back to the topic at hand. Be patient and understanding.

Negators This description refers to the faultfinders and nay-sayers. When they criticize you, use one of the neutralizing statements discussed on the next page and proceed with the point you want to make. Be especially careful to keep your reply related to the job.

How to Defuse Disagreement

Disagreement of any kind is never pleasant to experience. It can come at you in many ways, some that are innocent, some that are not. Follow these techniques and you should become more proficient in dealing with disagreement whenever it occurs.

If you offer an opinion the interviewer doesn't share, take these steps to regain rapport: Acknowledge that the interviewer may not share your views and that you appreciate his or her telling you so and being willing to hear what you have to say. Immediately bridge back to areas of agreement and reestablish common bonds while minimizing your differences.

Never debate viewpoints. Instead, bridge your response to the most positive and relevant point you can make and quickly end it on that note. In trying to get back to more productive areas, you might consider the help you can gain from such neutralizers as these:

"I understand how you feel about. . . ."

"I might well believe that, too, if that had been my experience."

"You certainly have a right to think that, based on what you heard previously."

Remember that every question is an opportunity. Use it as one.

Why Interviewers Resist

- They distrust ideas that differ from their own.
- They may distrust your motives.
- They may lack personal convictions.
- They may want to avoid being told what to do.
- They may feel a need to prove their power.
- They may fear repercussions from their superiors.
- They may be in a bad mood or a bad situation.
- They may not want to relinquish territory.
- They may not like something about you or about what you are saying.
- They may prefer the status quo.
- They may have better ideas!

Stripping Difficult Questions

Whether a difficult question is a setup, an attempt to box you in, a matter of personal style, or just an unfortunate choice of words, you are going to have to deal with it. Don't let such a question bother you. As always, go for the win-win response.

The technique for responding to a difficult question is a bit complex, but you can use it with many other types of questions:

- Listen carefully to the question, pause, and then isolate the loaded aspect or the part you don't like.
- Determine the actual issue.
- Consider how you might neutralize the question.
- Select a way to begin your response that will show empathy and also buy a few seconds of thinking time.

For example, suppose someone asks, "Would you say your former employer was actually ripping off employees' pensions by finding reasons to dump them?"

Avoid the trap. Remain calm and put your emotional energies into the intellectual game that faces you. Ask yourself the questions we've discussed.

What words sent up the red flags? "Ripping off" and "dump."

What's at issue here? Ethical business practices.

How can I strip this down to a neutral question? Address the issue, not the words.

How can I begin with an empathetic statement that also gains time to put my thoughts in order? Start by acknowledging the individual's emotions, position, or view.

Here's how the answer might sound:

- Begin with an opener such as one of the following:
- "You evidently have a strong view on what took place, Fred." "I can respect your views on that, Fred." "That is one way of looking at it, Fred."
- Go on to say something like this: "And if I understand you correctly, the issue is whether the company behaved unethically."
- Without hesitation, continue by saying something like: "On that issue, I can't comment, because I don't know enough of the details to judge."
- Without pause, continue by saying: "I would be more interested in knowing about the future. Can you tell me about *your* company's pension program and how participants are protected?"

You have responded within a reasonable time and you have also redirected the conversation to a more relevant point. Most significantly, you have displayed an ability not to be mousetrapped, to have grace under pressure, and to steer the interview back in a more productive direction.

By Popular Demand

Not all difficult questions can be identified by the way they are phrased. Some are difficult simply because they represent an effort to elicit information that you would prefer not to disclose. Take this one, for example: "Are you considering any other offers right now? What can you tell me about them?"

Earlier, we said that honesty is not only the best policy; it's the *only* policy. We'll stand by that, even here, but you can be truthful in many ways. For example, if you have other jobs under consideration, say so, but do it this way: "I have been talking with other employers. But since I don't know whether their search is confidential, I'd prefer not to mention any names." This shows you are a thoughtful, mature person who can respect proprietary information. Those are attributes any employer should desire.

If you prefer, you can go another way by saying: "At the moment, the position you and I are discussing is the only one I'm thinking about." This also should be true. If it isn't, you shouldn't be there.

The rule? Be courteous on touchy questions, but don't tell more than you have to.

How to Gain Thinking Time

Before you answer some of the more difficult questions, you may want time to contemplate your response. If you need time, just tell the interviewer so: "George, that's something that deserves a considered answer. Can we come back to it?" Or you might ask the interviewer to elaborate on the question, which will give you additional input as well as time to think.

Moving Beyond Disagreement

If you want the job, you won't get it if you are only responsive and responsible, admirable though that may sound. Most interviewers find such an attitude to be too passive, and they will expect more from you if you want to stay in the race.

Some of the techniques that follow can even help you take control of the interview, but that doesn't mean you should. It might be better for everyone if you limit your use of these techniques to planting the seeds for constructive recall and follow-up.

The following techniques can help you stand out from the crowd and keep the interview moving toward your goal. We mentioned one or two of them earlier in another context. Here we will consider them as ways to keep your target sharply in focus so you can use them whenever you feel they would be appropriate.

Future Pacing "Once we finish our discussion, you may want to consider how closely my credentials fit this opening." The key to the success of this technique lies in our ability to discuss possibilities as though they were realities, since the subconscious mind is unable to distinguish reality from fantasy. Thus, when you can persuade someone to think of something *as though* it were an actuality, so that he or she subconsciously accepts it as such, you will increase the chance that the mind will loop back, accept the suggestion, and act on it *as though* it were already fact.

Upon hearing the suggestion, "you may *want to consider how closely my credentials fit this opening,"* the interviewer's mind is likely to go through this process and, indeed, do just that. After all, it's something the interviewer already knows how to do, and he or she is going to have to do it with some candidates anyway. Thus, the suggestion is reasonable enough, isn't it? In its objective, it is not much different from saying, "I'd like you to consider me for the job," but that is more obvious and could meet with resistance. The future-paced statement, on the other hand, gives you a better opportunity to have the same idea receive the interviewer's consideration.

Embedment "It may be possible that *you have seen enough candidates to make your decision."* On a conscious level, the interviewer hears you express your own views in a very speculative manner: "It may be. . . ." On an embedment level, however, the interviewer's subconscious hears: *". . . you have seen enough candidates to make your decision."* By presenting the thought in a way that is comfortable to your interviewer, you increase the chance of acceptance. It is a powerful tool for overcoming resistance and helping the interviewer keep you in mind. Like so many advanced techniques, it is neutral until it is used. The rest is up to the user.

Reframing "It might cost you a little more in salary to bring me in at this time, but my organizational skills could save you at least the equivalent of another half person in the department." The technique says: "There is another way to look at this." It takes a seeming negative, your salary in this case, and puts it in a positive context: the savings that would come about.

Linking "You know, Harry, it's just a matter of having a non-profit background and the skills that are needed on this job." In this case, the interviewer was looking for corporate, not non-profit, experience. Using the linking technique enables you to gain acceptance for an idea that might be difficult to sell otherwise. It works because when you put two ideas together, the second tends to give support to the first. Because you have connected them, they seem interconnected. That helps make the first one more acceptable to the interviewer.

Giving "Permission" "You know, Tom, it's okay to think about engineering skills and supervisory talent in the same context." Even though the interviewer may have expressed a concern over it, the candidate's heavy engineering background has now been put into a new context. The technique is to link two concepts that the listener may have previously found incompatible. It is so obvious that it may appear to be ineffective, which partially explains its power. It enables you to give the interviewer "permission" to think in a way that may have been contrary to his or her views. Since people recall so very little of what they hear anyhow, you help the interviewer retain what you give permission to consider. Just be sure you have examples, anecdotes, or proof of some other kind to show how it really is "okay."

Other Techniques Of course, other techniques are available, thanks to research in the behavioral sciences. Check the reading list at the end of this book for titles.

Additional Rapport

In your interviews, be sure to use the matching techniques described in Chapter 12 for establishing a better rapport. One of the most effective uses of this technique is the "bridging" concept touched on earlier, in which you try to match the interviewer's word choices (visual, auditory, or kinesthetic), rate of speech, voice tones, pitch, intensity, inflections, and accent. These step-by-step details can help you carry out the bridging technique even with a difficult interviewer:

- Observe and reflect the interviewer's own words, voice tones, body language, and other patterns, so that they can flow smoothly through you from their present mode (visual, auditory, or tactile) to others.
- To accomplish this, first reflect the questioner's present mode, whether indicated through verb choice, speech rate, breathing, or another manner. Then start with readily agreeable, general observations and observe the individual's responses. Again pace his or her verb choices, speech rate, breathing, and other responses and switch to another sensory mode.
- Observe the questioner's response. Match that again and then switch into another mode.
- If the questioner fails to make the switch with you or if you observe resistance or lack of interest at any point, immediately shift back to the original mode where interest was high. If he or she objects, acknowledge the concern directly, and then shift back. If the person is indecisive, return to where receptivity was highest, elicit agreement, and then try switching again.
- Once you have engaged all three modes, you should be able to achieve greater understanding and acceptance.
- This technique may help you in situations where, in the past, you may not have received the acceptance you felt was merited.

Your Best Shot

By knowing as much as possible about the organization, the opening, and your own skills before the interview, you can use your rehearsals to prepare yourself to anticipate the questions and get behind the résumé to show how well you would fit the opening. You can learn how to take complete charge of yourself and your answers.

Reread the guidance in Chapter 7 on how to rehearse, and take time to practice the techniques before you walk into an employment interview.

17
How to Avoid Misunderstandings

Many questions are not what they seem. When you hear them, you think you understand them, only to learn later on that your meaning may not have been the interviewer's. Sometimes this occurs because the interviewer assumes that you absolutely must know what he or she is talking about. If that perception is inaccurate, it will be up to you to find out what you need to know.

Most of these semantic problems occur when the words used can have more than one meaning, no meaning, or any meaning the speaker or listener chooses to assign. The examples and suggestions that follow should help you come up with responses that will be more helpful to each of you. (The concept is not phrased as you should respond.)

PROBLEM: *Information Is Missing*
STATEMENT: "Your résumé is not very achievements-oriented."
PROBE CONCEPT: What specifically makes you feel that way?

PROBLEM: *You Don't Know to Whom or to What the Speaker Refers*
STATEMENT: "I find this to be stretching things a little."
PROBE CONCEPT: What is it you're having difficulty with?

PROBLEM: *You Don't Know What Is Being Compared*
STATEMENT: "The academic part of your background could be better."
PROBE CONCEPT: Better than what? In what way?

162

PROBLEM: *The Action Is Not Clear*
STATEMENT: "You seem to have involved yourself in a lot."
PROBE CONCEPT: How do you mean that? In what way?

PROBLEM: *The Questioner Turns a Process into an Event*
STATEMENT: "The committee will have to make the final decision."
PROBE CONCEPT: In your view, what criteria will they use?

PROBLEM: *The Questioner Reads Minds*
STATEMENT: "Everyone knows that. . . ."
PROBE CONCEPT: How can we be sure what *every*one thinks?

PROBLEM: *The Source of the Belief or Opinion Is Unclear*
STATEMENT: "Some say this kind of experience may be a disadvantage today."
PROBE CONCEPT: Who says this?

PROBLEM: *The Cause and Effect Are Unclear*
STATEMENT: "The absence of a master's may create problems for you."
PROBE CONCEPT: How is that likely to happen?

PROBLEM: *Imperative Statements Are Made (Must, need to, have to, cannot, unable, etc.)*
STATEMENT: "You need to have at least three years' experience doing. . . ."
PROBE CONCEPT: What would be the outcome if I just don't have that, but could offer something else just as good?

PROBLEM: *The Statement Is Overblown*
STATEMENT: "Regulators always say that about our company."
PROBE CONCEPT: What are they saying? Under what circumstances?

More Rehearsal

Write down the questions you might get in each of the above categories and then practice your responses aloud. Always phrase your replies so that they will be most acceptable to your interviewer and will encourage elaboration. Watch your voice tones.

This is also the time to jot down anything else you might encounter or that has confronted you in previous interviews. Doing so now will give you the practice you need to be at your best when such a situation arises in the future.

Listening with a Purpose

If you find yourself speaking more than the interviewer, you may be saying too much. We have all heard that the person who listens holds more power than the person who tells. Sometimes, though, the problem is one of not knowing *how* to listen.

It will be to your advantage to pay genuine attention at all times to what the interviewer tells you. Gather every bit of information you can on what life on the job would be like. Later on, you will need this input to make a better decision. Listening carefully will give you the opportunity to determine the best ways to respond to whatever you hear. It will also enable you to tailor your responses to address the interviewer's needs.

WHAT THE INTERVIEWER IS SAYING

One of the problems with listening—really listening—is that we often assume we know what the other person means, and we tune out part of our minds so that we can rehearse what we want to say next. In the process, we often fall victim to misunderstanding. We frequently act as though an employment interview were comprised of a person who asks questions and a person who answers them. That is anything but true. As you have seen, you have a right, even an obligation, to ask questions. However, you also have a need to listen carefully to whatever you hear.

A Point to Ponder

There are thousands of words in the dictionary, millions of ways to combine words into sentences, and perhaps hundreds of millions of ways to combine sentences into paragraphs. Of all those possibilities, your interviewer has chosen to say whatever he or she has said.

That is fact. It is your input, your raw data for something even more important. It is your basis for understanding. Might you wonder why, out of myriad possibilities, your interviewer chose to make a particular statement? If you do, you have taken the first step toward becoming a careful listener. Consider a statement as seemingly innocuous as this one: "This job requires someone who can handle several projects at once," says the interviewer.

There it is, simple enough. So simple that the common, knee-jerk reaction is usually to try to respond immediately with something like this: "Oh, I have to do a lot of that in my present job. As a matter of fact . . ." When you launch into this monologue, you have lost a major opportunity. First of all, as we have seen, words constitute less than 10 percent of the total communication in any dialogue. Visual and auditory input comprise the rest. What we see and how we hear provide the input for how we feel about things. Some other things to consider are that:

- People respond best to those who really listen nonjudgmentally.
- You don't learn anything new when it's your voice that's doing the talking.
- Most of what you tell the interviewer will be forgotten before the day has ended.

What survive the process are impressions. "Did I like this candidate? Would the candidate fit in well here?" Those questions far outweigh the raw facts, especially since most job seekers who reach the candidate level have comparable skills. Otherwise they wouldn't have made it through the screening process.

If impressions are that important and listening has a higher value than speaking, why not get behind the speaker's words and try to learn more? Think about the interviewer's statement again: "This job requires someone who can handle several projects at once."

Your Options

The interviewer must have told you that for a reason. Interviews are brief; time is precious; no message is without meaning. It will be up to you to discover what's behind the words. Here are your most valuable options for doing so. You can:

- Explore the interviewer's statement in more depth
- Seek to learn the intentions behind telling you this
- Learn the interviewer's feelings on the matter
- Find out what this means to him or her
- Determine what actions the interviewer feels are appropriate

Let's take those possibilities one at a time and see how you might respond if you were to make each of the choices.

1. Explore the interviewer's statement in more depth: "Greta, I wonder if you could be a little more specific. What kinds of projects would be involved here?"

2. Seek to learn the intentions behind telling you this: "Greta, I appreciate your sharing that with me. Could you tell me what it might mean to me on the job?"
3. Learn the interviewer's feelings on the matter: "Greta, you certainly know more about that than I do. How do you feel about it?"
4. Find out what this means to him or her: "Greta, could you help me understand how this might be important on the job?"
5. Determine what actions the interviewer feels are appropriate: "Greta, in light of what you're saying, what actions would be expected of me in that context?"

DEFYING TRADITION

Now compare any of these options with the traditional rejoinder that most people would have come up with: "Oh, I have to do a lot of that in my present job. As a matter of fact . . ." What a difference.

Most of the words that might have been used to describe the kind of listening process detailed here have already been used by other authors: "active listening," "attentive listening," "creative listening," "emphatic listening," "reflective listening," and so on. So let's make up a handy label of our own for this kind of listening. Let's call it "care-full" listening, because every one of our optional responses provides the opportunity to show that you care about the job, about the interviewer, and about yourself.

In each case, you are seeking fuller understanding. This leaves less room for misinterpretation and prevents you from missing important input. Most of all, it shows your interviewer that you are a thoughtful, courteous individual who values other people's observations, opinions, and feelings.

When you use the technique, recognize that you don't have to limit yourself to a single option: You can always explore the interviewer's initial statement of fact from as many angles as each of you feels would be profitable.

18
Special Considerations

No matter how much you try to plan and anticipate, there will always be something more to consider. Certain kinds of interviews, for example, don't fit the one-on-one mold completely. In this chapter you'll find the exceptions you are most likely to encounter.

Group Meetings

An interview in which you are meeting more than one person at a time need not take on the overtones of an inquisition. Generally, such an interview is held for these reasons: to save screening time in looking at the better candidates, to enable each interviewer to pick up on points that the others may have overlooked, and to provide a fuller picture of the organization for the candidate.

Since a group interview requires special preparation and a particular strategy for success, always ask these questions when the appointment is made: Who will be present at the interview? Will I be meeting others? At the same time? In successive interviews on the same day? How much time should I bracket for this appointment or series of appointments?

At the same time, ask the name and title of each person. Finally, ask the reporting relationships and how each person fits into the organizational chart. Write the names and titles (and departments if different) on an index card in order of reporting relationships. Clip the card to the top of the yellow legal pad that you will keep in front of you during the meeting. When you get into the interview, code each individual from left to right on your card. (You may wish to draw a diagram to make this more clear.) The card might look like this:

---

1 Leslie Wood, VP Marketing (to whom the position reports)
2 Jane Pearson, VP Sales (parallel position to Wood's)
3 Tom Settle, Director of Marketing (your equal)
4 John Correll, Personnel Administrator (for the department)

WHO'S IN CHARGE

One person will generally set the agenda of a group interview and host the meeting. The session might be held in the host's office, a conference room, or a restaurant. (More about this latter situation in a moment.)

Since group interviews often occur as second meetings, you are likely to have already met the person who will run the meeting. If this is not a second appointment, you may have been through an initial screening by that individual before being introduced to the others.

In either case, this is not an inquisition. In fact, it's an opportunity. By practicing the same nonverbal skills discussed earlier, including posture, eye contact, and voice tones, you have the opportunity to make a favorable impression on several people at the same time. This is actually easier on the psyche than trying to maintain a high level of performance while being led through sequential interviews with different people.

The social amenities will be predictably brief, and the meeting will generally begin with an overview by the host—in this case, Leslie Wood. She may also set set some ground rules about who will speak or ask questions and when you will have the opportunity yourself to speak or question.

If you are to sit in a lounge area with chairs and a sofa, try to seat yourself in one of the chairs. Besides the previously mentioned disadvantages of sofas and low seats, sitting on a sofa in a group interview is likely to put you sideways to at least one of the interviewers, or even worse, between two of them. A separate seat need not be the hot seat: In this case, it can become the director's chair.

If you are to sit at a rectangular conference table, sit opposite your interviewers for the same reason. If you are to sit at a round table, try to position yourself with your back to a solid wall rather than a doorway. In either situation, avoid facing bright sunlight.

As you maintain your alert and attentive posture, be sure to look at the person who is speaking or to whom you are speaking, even if that person is not looking at you. Convey your interest in what is being said at all times. That is especially important when the speaker is being supportive. Also, doing so can help keep everyone focused on the speaker rather than on you. It shows you to be a courteous person.

DOWN TO BUSINESS

The business of the interview starts with the first question, usually asked by the host. Remember, though, you're still buying, so remain assertive. If you haven't yet been given the specifics of the opening, you will need them now so that you can participate effectively. You need to know as much as the others do about what you're there to talk about, so ask for the information. Here's how.

"It might be appropriate," you begin diplomatically, sharing your eye contact with everyone as you continue, "for you first to describe the position more fully. Then I can be more responsive and make the best use of everyone's time. Could someone do that, please?" Look directly at the host as you conclude. It's her show, and you would not have been introduced to the others unless there was some desire to see you succeed. She has a stake in your doing well at this point.

Once the job is described for you, most likely by the host, who is the department's vice president, thank her. You are taking charge, but in a most appropriate manner.

If no one advances a question right away, follow through with something like this: "I appreciate your giving me this opportunity to learn more about the position. Would this be a good time for someone to tell me how it fits into the departmental scheme of things?" As you end, look at Correll. As the personnel representative here, he should take over the ball now. He may turn to Wood for a nonverbal go-ahead, and then start to speak.

If you have been able to carry this scheme forward this far, you are fortunate. Usually at this point, if not before, the discussion may become more free-form, or Wood may initiate a question or ask others for their questions.

Keep in mind that you haven't heard from two others in the meeting yet: Jane Pearson and Tom Settle. Does your position interface with sales? Does the director of marketing report to you, or work with you? You need to know. It is important to clarify the reporting relationships in terms of responsibility, accountability, and authority. Do it now, before you are hired. Don't wait until it's too late and then find you have problems getting your job done because of the way the chain of command is structured.

As the interview proceeds, everyone should take turns speaking and listening. The old adage about people having two ears, two eyes, and one mouth comes to mind here. Listen carefully and fully. Take notes. Answer each question completely according to the guidelines covered previously, but don't volunteer more than you were asked.

Thirty minutes gives you time for only fourteen questions or so in a one-on-one interview; even an hour gives each participant time for only a few questions in a group interview. And, of course, the more people who participate, the fewer questions each can ask.

Don't hesitate to ask the other participants specific but friendly questions about their functions. They will be answering in front of their colleagues and they are almost obliged to respond, so this can be a real opportunity to learn about your potential coworkers.

One candidate who did ask questions had learned through his personal contacts during the research phase that the department had a serious problem with one employee and no one seemed to be dealing with it. The candidate used the group interview situation pointedly to ask the individual's supervisor (who would be reporting to the candidate if hired): "Since it would be to everyone's benefit to exercise honesty and candor with anyone you plan to hire, can you tell me about any personnel situations in your area that I should know about in considering this opening—while still respecting individuals' rights of privacy, of course?"

The candidate proceeded through the question at an even, carefully modulated pace, never breaking eye contact. When he finished, he remained silent. The supervisor fidgeted. The host exchanged glances with him. The supervisor answered the question.

STICK TO THE ISSUE
No matter where the questions may roam, keep your responses sharply focused on giving out information that will enhance your cause. Address the topic, but always bring your answer "back home," as we discussed in Chapter 16.

You should never be at a disadvantage in a group interview, or in any other kind, when you have done your homework. Although more people may be present, they can ask you only so many questions in a given time period. Besides, you know a lot about them and can use that knowledge to learn even more, just as you would in a one-on-one meeting. You also know yourself inside and out by now. Your planning and rehearsals have prepared you to respond to any question with the details that will bring you closer to the job at hand.

Luncheon Interviews

Lunches can be an opportunity or a nuisance. Many candidates don't like luncheon meetings, particularly when they have not prepared very well and are unable to ask questions that will keep the interviewer talking enough for them to eat. Which brings us to these points: Taking an interview without preparing for it is like starting on a trip without putting gas in the car. One should not assume that the purpose of a lunch interview is to eat.

FOOD CONSIDERATIONS
Order food that (1) you are familiar with and have eaten before, (2) fits in with what your host is ordering, (3) can be delivered to the table quickly, (4) needs little or no carving, (5) is easy to get onto your fork, (6) won't slide off your fork or spoon, (7) won't drip, (8) can be pushed around on your plate (to look as though you've eaten more than you've had a chance to), and (9) won't cause you instant indigestion.

If you are invited to order a drink, remember the rule that you should never do anything alone. In this case, go one step further. Instead of saying "I will if you're having one," say "If you're having something, I'll have an iced tea [Pepsi, Perrier . . .]." Make no excuses. Even if you might like a glass of wine or something stronger, this is not the time to indulge. You need to be at your sharpest for the interview that brought you there.

Facing Interruptions

Although I mentioned interruptions in Chapter 9 as part of the problem of being kept waiting, other aspects need to be considered. You might want to believe that the interviewer has locked in your entire appointment time so there can be absolutely no interruptions, but logic is against it. Things do happen. The only question to consider is this: How do you and the interviewer deal with the interruptions when they do occur? Let's start with the interviewer.

The interviewer who will accept interruptions to sign letters, handle phone calls, and say hello to colleagues who stick their heads in the door is not focusing on the interview. The meeting that can influence your future just doesn't have the same priority for the interviewer. That is unfortunate, but it reflects upon your host, not upon you. If this person is ultimately to become your boss, you can expect more of the same treatment. In such an interview, simply pause each time you are interrupted and when you start again, backtrack with a quick summary of the point you were trying to make.

If you arrive at the meeting to find that the interviewer has higher priorities, such as a report that "has to be in the boss's hands by three o'clock," you may be watching a poor planner at work. If the interviewer would be your boss, let that guide your decision. Perhaps you'll get lucky and your priorities will rank as high on his desk—even higher than he apparently ranks his invited guests.

Unexpected company is a different issue: If you are meeting with the VP of a regional office and the president of the parent organization walks in unannounced, you can be certain the interviewer will interrupt your meeting to say hello. Most likely the interviewer will explain that you are being interviewed and set a cutoff time for your appointment in order to meet with the boss. It is just as likely that the president will understand. If, however, they need to transact some business, offer to step out of the office without waiting to be asked. They'll appreciate your thoughtfulness. When your meeting resumes, however, each of you may have to summarize what you had discussed prior to the interruption.

If a true crisis strikes, deal with it the best way you can. You must put the interview out of your mind. Don't become desperate as one candidate did: The interviewer received a call that his wife was on the way to the hospital to have their first child. As he tried to leave to be with her, the job seeker followed him to the elevator that never came and then down three flights of stairs while spouting his reasons why he thought he should be hired. The boss, on the other hand, knew one good reason why he shouldn't be.

Test-Taking

There are two kinds of tests that might take place during your interview: Skills tests and personality-aptitude tests. You will generally have to take skills tests to get a job for which they are relevant. You can also ask to take them at another time, and you don't have to offer much of a reason for doing so, either. I know of an employee who was hired immediately when she said with a smile, "I'm sure it's important for you to know how well I can use this computer, but I'd like to do this at another time, *because* I'll be more relaxed than I am right now in our interview. That way you'll have a better idea of how *my work will meet your standards.*" (Italicized words indicate embedments; see Chapters 12 and 16.)

It was a fair request. The interviewer liked everything he had learned about the candidate's qualifications, and he decided she couldn't have gotten that far without the requisite skills on the computer. He was right, as she demonstrated in her first week on the job.

Psychological testing is another matter. Many employers would be attracted to a test that would tell them what kinds of people fit best in which environments. So far, however, there are no silver bullets of sufficient accuracy, or that can tell the employer whether the individual will be effective *on the job.* Stories abound about employers who have totally disregarded the findings of such tests, hired the candidates anyway, and been well satisfied with their decisions.

On another level, I would have to question the right of an organization to probe something so private as an outsider's personality by using testing tools that are of questionable validity and that are subject to interpretation by a test reader whose credentials may be marginal. Consider this: If the instrument is perceived to be valid, using it is tantamount to an invasion of privacy, because such testing would normally occur in the privacy of a licensed psychologist's office. If the organization doesn't perceive it to be valid, why is it used at all? In my opinion, candidates have the moral right, and should have the legal right, to refuse to take such tests. This view, of course, does not apply to aptitude tests, civil service examinations, and comparable tests designed to help predict one's potential to succeed in a given field based on ability.

Illegal Questions

Yes, there is a federal law that governs what employers are *not* entitled to ask you, but the law is not without its loopholes and exceptions. Commonly referred to as Title VII (the Civil Rights Act of 1964, and its amendments), the law pertains only to companies with fifteen or more employees. It also leaves room for employers who have a need to know certain information for job-related reasons.

Most employers realize that race, sex, and religion are taboo subject areas; that is the basis for the equal employment opportunity legislation. If you know the law and are familiar with your rights, what should you do if you are asked an illegal question? Do you declare the question out of bounds? Leave? File a lawsuit? Assuming you are correct and the employer has no legal right to ask the question, will it make a difference if he or she did not know which questions are off limits? Will it matter that he or she may have had a reasonable purpose in asking the question?

In one case with which I am familiar, the employer asked a female applicant what she would do with her year-old child during working hours. (She had volunteered information about the baby.) Although the interviewer's firm had fewer than fifteen employees and so he was not restricted legally from asking the question, this was not the issue: His reason, it turned out, was that until the candidate had made day-care arrangements, he was willing to invite her to bring her child to the office when she could not find a sitter.

Some things have to be put in proper perspective. One candidate mentioned something about her church activities. The employer, also a church-goer, asked what church she went to. Was it an illegal question, or was it an effort to show an interest and establish a rapport? The business did have over fifteen employees, after all. The point here is not to demean legislation that serves a valid purpose. It is simply to say that there are times when an extra bit of understanding on the candidate's part may help the situation succeed for all parties.

"Are you living with someone?" *may* be an illegal question, but what if it's asked by one man of another merely to extend an offer to join an apartment-sharing group with other men his age?

"Do you have a criminal record?" may be illegal to ask in most instances but not if you have valid, job-related reasons for asking. The intent of the law is to protect people who, historically, have been discriminated against. If you feel you need to report a potential employer, do so. You'll most likely get immediate action. You may not get the job, however, and even if you do, you may not receive a very enthusiastic welcome.

Instead, try this approach to see if you can get behind the question and discover intent. When you are asked what you feel may be an illegal question, respond by saying: "That's an unexpected question, and I'm sure you must have a reason for it. Would you please elaborate for me?" What you hear next will either reassure you of the interviewer's good intentions or let the interviewer get into deep trouble. When I shared this concept with an attorney in this field, she said: "I like it."

In many cases, if you can anticipate an area that might be of reasonable concern to a potential employer, you might broach the subject yourself and let the interviewer know why your candidacy would not be affected.

Once you've gotten this far through the interview successfully, you are ready for the next step: closing the meeting.

19
Closing the Meeting

In Chapter 8, we talked about the three parts of the interview. Now it's time to consider that third part—saying goodbye—in more detail.

After your first interview with an employer, you are not likely to receive a job offer before you leave. The employer will need to evaluate other candidates who have already been interviewed, compare notes with others within the organization, and possibly interview more applicants.

Even once you are selected, the process hasn't ended. For example, the organization will need to run you through personnel before you're hired. Think about those words: "before you're hired." Never lose sight of the fact that you don't have the job until you're in the job. You will be evaluated in everything you do and for every step you take. So continue to be the best *you* that you can be at all times.

A Successful Close

You learned earlier what takes place during the final stage of the interview. Keep in mind, however, that anything can still happen. Since saying goodbye can have its awkward moments, focus intently on the process. I have seen candidates' apprehension levels suddenly rise out of nowhere, causing some strange things to happen. One individual who found herself juggling briefcase and purse suddenly decided to shake my hand. In her self-imposed frustration, she grasped my thumb instead of my whole hand. To her credit, she recognized that she had lost control momentarily and looked at me with a smile that said, "Oh well." As she set her briefcase on the floor and put her purse over her shoulder, she said, "Now. Can we try that one more time?" We did. And it worked.

Goodbyes can be even more harrowing than that. One hapless soul who had been in a conference room meeting to try to sell some audio-visual equipment finished his closing remarks, shook everyone's hand, turned away from the conference table, and strode purposefully through the door—right into a large closet.

Take charge of everything you do, and you shouldn't have to concern yourself with problems such as those. Instead, you will be able to focus on whatever else you need to know before you leave and to handle the rest of your departure well.

Finding Out Where You Stand

As the interview shifts into the final stage, it will ease your stress to know what might happen next. If the interview has gone well, which it should have, you are ready to find out where you stand. You can accomplish this through any number of trial closes. The close of any sales presentation usually involves more words in the tactile mode than in either of the other two modes. Here are some you might consider:

"It seems we might have a good *match* here. Would you agree?"

"Would it be to your benefit *to have someone* with my skills [background, experience, . . .] on this project?"

"How would you feel about being able *to take care* of this problem [one that has received prime attention in the meeting] to your satisfaction?"

"It would be great to *work together*, wouldn't it?"

The tactile mode is preferred for most closing situations, but if your interviewer is transmitting in an auditory or visual mode, you will have to match that first. Then you can shift back to one of the closes recommended above. Here are some visual examples followed by auditory ones:

"It *looks* like we have a good match here. Would you agree?"

"We really have a *clear picture* of things as they might look on the job, haven't we?"

"This *looks* like a real opportunity for both of us, doesn't it?"

"The whole idea *sounds* good from almost every perspective, doesn't it?"

"I'm eager to *discuss* the next step, aren't you?"

Maintain the Right Attitude

You might wonder whether some of these sound a bit pushy. If you feel that way about particular ones, you are probably right in not using them yourself. Instead, develop your own, ones you can feel comfortable using. Don't let a momentary discomfiture interfere with your purpose, however. You are there to help both you and the employer find out if you make a good match. If things went even reasonably well, there is nothing wrong with finding out as much of the answer as you can.

The key to success here rests with the attitude you convey. If you *sound* pushy or act pushy, you are more likely to be perceived that way. If you remain courteous and ask in a professional way, that is how you will be seen. Before you get too far into your closing, be sure to let the interviewer know that you appreciate the time you have been given to explore this opportunity. You should also briefly discuss any "mechanical" details you need to wrap up, such as how to submit your expenses if the employer has agreed to underwrite your visit.

Planting the Seeds for Follow-up

Leave open the opportunity to call the interviewer sometime in the near future. Your purpose will be to keep track of your status. What you say now should go something like this: "I'm sure we can feel free to contact one another on anything else that might occur to us. Is that okay with you?" That's all you need to say in order to retain the opportunity to check back in a few days or so.

As you leave, there maybe more need for small talk, say, if the interviewer or the secretary walks you to an elevator or lobby. It would be a mistake to loop back into any of your business discussion, because that could leave you with an awkward "Well anyway, thanks," closure. If the interviewer reverts to a point made in the interview, try to help keep it confined. You will need a response that shuts down the possibility of further discussion without making you sound abrupt. For that, you might consider saying something like "Well, that is certainly something to consider." Then swing right back into your departure small talk.

Before you go, be sure to thank the secretary by name for helping to make the appointment possible. He or she may have handled the arrangements for you, set up the interview, helped you with your coat, brought you coffee, kept potential intruders away, and more. Most important, the secretary is your key to further access to the interviewer.

One more time, after everything else has been said and just before you leave, look at the people who say goodbye to you and say, "I *appreciate* your time."

20
Your Reactions

While the interview with, say, Steve Wilkins is still prominent in your thoughts, jot down as much information as you can. What are his likes and interests? Hobbies? Personal strengths on the job? What did you like in him as a potential supervisor? What did you notice about his office that made it special or that said something personal about him? What was said about things you may need to do next? What have you been asked to send? To whom? Whom are you supposed to call? When? About what?

Record all that while you are still thinking about it and before you take any other interviews. Remember what happened to the person who looked at several sofas in several stores without taking notes. This is also the time to record your impressions about all aspects of the job. For starters, ask yourself these questions:

What do you like or dislike about the job? Although you made your best efforts to gain as much information as possible during the interview, you may still not know whether your initial impressions would prove accurate if you were to try to learn more. Write down what you liked and disliked, but be aware that both the pros and the cons could change and try to check out your feelings as you gain further information.

What, in particular, would make you a good candidate? With an accurate assessment of the organization, the department, and the job, you should be able to gauge the attributes that you would be able to bring into the position. Were your interviewers especially interested in leadership skills? Which ones? Were they more interested in your accomplishments? On which achievements did they focus? Did they stress your skills as a team player? Which skills were most important?

How did you feel about the physical facilities? You will be spending approximately one-quarter of your life in this environment. Will you be glad to come in every day? Is it where you want to spend your business life? Your surroundings must be comfortable if you expect to do your best work. For example, some people aren't cut out to function in an offices-without-walls environment. Others may not enjoy a private office if it is too small and confining.

Would you want to work here? What is your gut feeling? Setting aside your need for a job, if that is your situation, ask yourself that very question: "Would I really want to work here?" Listen carefully to the answer. It's your career.

What about the reporting and supervisory relationships? It is amazing how many candidates walk away from the first interview believing that they know enough about who reports to whom. On the job, many have found that they didn't ask enough questions or didn't ask the right ones. Your interviewer may not want to disclose privileged information, but you will need to know precisely who reports to whom and whether that reporting relationship is a solid line (clear-cut) or dotted line (latch-string) on the organizational chart. If it's latchstring, you may find that this individual, or someone else, has a different concept of the relationship. And it may not be to your benefit.

Are the people to your liking? You don't have to like everyone in the world, nor will everyone always like you. The real question is, can you get along with them? Again, you may need more input. This is where a second interview will work to your advantage. It will give you the opportunity to discover what you need to know about the people who will surround you.

What would Wilkins be like as a boss? Were you able to determine whether Wilkins is what you need in a boss? Will he be critical or never be around? Will he provide leadership, be supportive, set realistic goals and schedules, enjoy working with *you?*

Will the job provide what you need to be successful? Perhaps, before your first interview, you gave little thought to what you might need in a job in order to feel successful. You may just have wanted a job, period. After one or two interviews, however, job seekers often begin to reflect on this more. It seems that, just as often, they try to stifle their thoughts about advancement because they may believe that such thinking would conflict with their first need: to become employed. Allow yourself to reflect on this: If the job won't fulfill your needs, the problem will come up sooner or later. Knowing where you want to go with your life helps set the course that will get you there.

What did you like or dislike about the interviewer? Did the interviewer have any particular characteristics that would be discomforting or annoying to you if you were to report to him? Here is a good time to consider such issues as smoking, drinking, language, attitudes, and viewpoints and opinions. Second interviews help candidates as well as employers in this area too.

When did you feel you were at your best in the interview? Was there a high point? A place where you were really all that you could be? What was that feeling? How did it come about? Can you get in touch with it again? Do so, if for no other reason than to fix positive interview experiences firmly in your mind. It will help you with mental rehearsals as you visualize transferring that success into future interviews.

How could you do better next time? Be kind to yourself here. There is no place for "could haves," "should haves," and "if onlys" in this evaluation. Simply address the areas where you did the best you could under the circumstances but where you would like to do better next time. These are the areas that you should specifically rehearse.

What do you think about the general tone of the organization? Tone is a difficult attribute to measure. Think of it as the way people treated one another. Did they smile and say hello to colleagues? Did they pause to exchange pleasantries, gestures, or acts of kindness? Or did they seem pressured, strained, and harried? Were they rude, antagonistic, or even hostile? In short, how can they be expected to treat the people with whom they come in contact?

What would your future be like in this organization? Perhaps the interviewer asked you where you see yourself in five or ten years. Ask yourself that question now. Do you know enough about the future of the organization, the department, or your future boss to know the answer? Don't assume anything. I have counselled executives whose companies have folded, whose departments have been downsized, whose jobs have been declared surplus, and whose bosses either broke or couldn't keep their prehiring promises.

Would this be a career position for you? More than another way to look at the same question, this one should start you thinking in more depth about where you are headed. Especially if you have had a spotty career record, you may want to start thinking now about whether accepting this position would merely lead you to more of what hasn't worked for you so far.

Do you know enough to make a prudent decision if the employer were to offer you the job? If not, what would you need to find out when you make the next contact with this employer? How could you learn more in the next interview with another organization?

What other reactions did you have? As you ponder these questions, write down any other reactions you may have had. Be as specific as you can, and resolve to check them out in a second interview if one becomes available, or before you accept an offer if the employer makes one.

Only a Beginning

Use this list as a starting point and expand upon it. The more input you have now, before you receive the offer, the more likely you are to make the right decision. Within a few days, either you will be calling the employer for additional information or you will receive a call that lets you know your status.

The above questions alone may not give you the depth of information you need in some areas. Some of the employer's responses may in fact be purposefully vague. Some employers may even give you the impression that they are annoyed with your questions. As we have said elsewhere in this book, attitudes belong to those who display them. They are not a reflection of you, your worth as an individual, or your right to ask questions. Remain tactful, however.

In some situations, even a reluctant employer has been known to give up information a candidate requested when it was asked for with the right attitude and followed with a reasonable explanation of how the information would help both parties arrive at the right decision.

If You Are Turned Down

If you are told you did not get the job, be careful not to blurt out, "Why not?" Questions that begin with the word "why" have overtones that would not serve you well here. The fact that an employer may decide not to hire you should not be construed as a judgment about you. If you do want to find out why, and feel poised enough to do so, you might try phrasing your question along these lines:

"I appreciate your telling me that, Fred. So I can benefit from the time you spent with me, would you mind sharing the thoughts you had in making your decision?"

The question could catch Fred off guard, so he might stall by saying, "What did you have in mind?" Should that happen, be prepared to follow

WHY CANDIDATES ARE TURNED DOWN

Despite your best efforts, you may learn that you are not being further considered for the opening. Accept what the employer tells you and remain courteous. In the job search process, never close a door so tightly that it cannot be opened at some later time.

The turndown may come despite your having gained the interview by the strength of your credentials, and it may be based on one of the following:

- Spotty employment record
- Lack of needed skills
- A managerial style in conflict with needs
- Unwillingness to accept the terms of employment
- Unwillingness to relocate
- A mismatch of personalities
- Attitude
- Salary expectations that are too high
- Unpreparedness for the interview
- Lack of tact or negotiating skills
- Lacks of potential for advancement
- Negative readings from references
- Another candidate seemed a better choice
- Search was put on hold

up with something such as: "Perhaps you could tell me what you found to be the pros and cons of our meeting."

A long silence could follow. If you avoid all temptation to fill the gap and let the interviewer speak next, you will be more likely to gain useful information. The chances are still not very good that he will level with you, but it's worth a try. He may tell you that other candidates happened to fit the company's needs better or even that the search has been "put on hold for the time being."

If he does volunteer anything more specific, he may confine his comments to the need for credentials that you either don't have or lack in depth. Most interviewers will try to get off the hook as graciously as possible and thus may not want to risk discussing anything more specific, out of concern that it might be misinterpreted or elicit a rebuttal.

If Fred does elect to give you some in-depth reasons why you were not selected, listen and be both grateful and gracious. His comments merely reflect personal needs and biases, and he is doing the best job possible in making a difficult decision. To try to refute what he tells you would be a mistake.

Arguing or offering counterpoints will not change the decision. Your only goal here should be to learn something and to leave the interviewer feeling good about knowing you. Again, it's a small world out there, and one never knows who might be interviewing whom in the future. Just close the conversation gracefully and continue to pursue your other leads.

How Interviewers Evaluate

Not all interviewers use formal rating scales to record their impressions of candidates. In fact, most may not. I am not familiar with any studies on the subject, but I would be surprised to learn that very many interviewers do much more than come up with decisions based on their feelings or the influence of others (their bosses, secretaries, and even outsiders) in making hiring decisions. Nonetheless, it might be useful to know some of the criteria they might use to evaluate candidates.

Of course, the initial impression you make is paramount. You will also be judged by the way you present yourself—your demeanor, attire, and grooming. How you handle the opening conversation is also important. An interviewer will, when recording initial reactions to you, consider the *way* you express yourself. Attitude is everything.

An interviewer will want to consider your long-term potential with the organization in terms of both your skills and your management style. How your personality might fit in will be another important factor.

Some of the characteristics that might be considered are whether you are a dominant or passive type, quiet or outgoing, positive or negative, people-oriented or a loner. The interviewer may also be thinking about whether you are confident or insecure, affable or overbearing, mature or immature.

She will certainly consider how she would feel if you worked for her day in and day out. In addition, she will match you up to other candidates in her mind, and possibly even to people who would be your peers on the job.

Note that little has been said about your credentials, and that's why the emphasis in any job search should not be on the résumé. What you put on paper must be right and it must reflect your skills, experience, and credentials, but its job is just to get you in the running. After that, everything is up to you.

Part Three
The Follow-up

21
How to Follow Up

One of the best ways to keep the door open for future dialogue is to follow up with a letter immediately. Don't wait a day or two to think about it. Here's why: If you met on a Tuesday and you don't mail your letter until Thursday, the letter probably won't reach the employer until the following Monday at the earliest. By then, a lot may have happened to diminish any impression you might have made.

Without appearing to be overeager—no overnight mail unless you were specifically asked to send it—get your letter onto the interviewer's desk as soon as you can. Mail it Tuesday afternoon and it may be received before the weekend. That will help reinforce a positive impression.

The follow-up letter is such a perfect opportunity to showcase one's favorable attributes that it amazes me more people don't use it. At the very least, the letter enables you to show that you are a thoughtful, courteous, and considerate individual who knows how to follow through.

Going Beyond the Norm

If you go beyond the vacuous form approach that most people use—if they write at all—you can do even more to showcase your ability to empathize with others. That is relatively easy to do when you follow the formula for such letters given on the following pages. I have provided both a sample letter and a general outline for one.

Dear Mr. Frankel:

It was a pleasure to meet with you on Tuesday, March 4, to discuss the position of Marketing Manager in your department.

It was interesting to learn that we both lived in Wisconsin and both enjoy cross-country skiing. As you will recall, it was in Wisconsin that I had the opportunity to work on the graphic design project that interested you in particular.

The position certainly sounds interesting, and I look forward to learning more about it. I am reviewing my notes on our meeting, and may want to call you within the next several days.

I look forward to speaking with you again soon.

Sincerely,

Leslie A. Arden

LAA:st

Travel Expenses

Generally, most organizations will cover your costs of getting to the meeting if they are beyond the average cab fare, but you should negotiate that before the interview. Customarily, expenses that an employer might willingly reimburse include transportation, meals, lodging, and minor but related items such as gratuities and parking fees.

If your prospective employer did agree to pay the expenses you incurred to attend the interview, this is the time to submit them. Even if you already know you are scheduled for a second interview, you should submit an invoice now if for no other reason than to keep your name in front of the interviewer. Do this as a postscript to your letter: "P.S. Thank you for your willingness to underwrite the costs of the trip for this interview. I have enclosed an invoice, together with all receipts." Sign your initials under the postscript.

INTERVIEW FOLLOW-UP LETTER

1. Address
2. Heading
3. Salutation
4. Express appreciation and mention the specific day, date, and month of interview.
5. Discuss any "special" details, both employment-related and personal. This section of the letter might touch lightly on specific details of the interview to show that you are serious about what transpired. Try to work in a comment about something of a social nature that was discussed during the interview. This could mean a reference to a hobby that you both enjoy, something personal or special that the two of you talked about, or even an unusual item that was on display in the office. As another alternative, you might share a comment about someone you both know (perhaps someone to whom you promised to say hello for the interviewer).
6. Relate your background as closely as possible to the job opening.
7. Close by expressing your desire to hear further from the employer.
8. Use "Sincerely,"
9. Signature
10. Type your name

The Invoice The invoice, like your résumés and letters, should look professional. Type it on bond paper (20 percent rag content preferred) and balance it on the page. Here again a computer or a word processor comes in handy. The layout of your expense form might look like the accompanying example.

Persevere Patiently

Not all good things happen overnight. It can take weeks for an employer to screen all prospects, check references, and carry out myriad other hiring details while juggling the regular office routine. Be patient, but persevere. Your initial follow-up letter was the first contact. Since it mentioned that you might call, it gives you an opportunity for the second contact. You should think the call through carefully before you make it, however.

REQUEST FOR REIMBURSEMENT

April 3, 1991

Submitted by: Laura Hanson
               32 Willow St.
               Ridgeville, IL

Purpose: Employment interview

Scheduled by: Nina Schwartz
               Sales Manager
               Thompson Technologies, Inc.

For: Expenses incurred for interview

Date: April 2, 1991

Item	Amount
TRANSPORTATION	
Airfare	$120.00
Taxi	$15.75
LODGING	
Hotel	$50.00
Gratuities	$10.00
Please pay this amount:	$195.75

(Note: Some organizations prefer that you use their own
expense forms rather than a form of your own. Ask about
this in advance.)

WHAT THE FOLLOW-UP CALL SHOULD DO

Many job seekers have told me that they failed to make any follow-up
calls because they didn't know what to say. As one woman put it, while
expressing her stress over just thinking about the call: "I mean, I just
can't call up the guy and say, 'Hey, did you decide to hire me or what?!?'"
Therein lies a dilemma: You know you shouldn't be that blunt, even

though you may be convinced that both you and the employer know what you *really* want when you call. So what do you do? What *do* you say when you call?

Prepare before you pick up the phone. Start by opening your prospect's folder and reviewing all your notes from the interview. Then review your first follow-up letter. This sequence enables you to pick up as many reminders of the meeting as possible before you home in on what you have already said. The homing in may give you a better focus, but if all you were to do was to read your follow-up letter before you call, you might not have enough information to handle a conversation shift into other topics you discussed at the meeting. On the other hand, looking at the letter just before you call helps remind you of the attitude you will need to help move the call along smoothly.

Once you have done your review, jot down any questions that you might want to discuss. Be sure to make them information-gathering in nature, and not too direct or pointed. You want to show an interest in the job, not get a ruling on whether you are still in the running.

This attitude is important. The prospect is unlikely to have a decision for you and therefore will not react well to pressure, perceived or otherwise. Make certain you keep the *tone* of the conversation relaxed and as friendly as possible. A relaxed and friendly tone does not mean rambling or attempting idle chit-chat. Your call should be brief, showing respect for the employer's time. It should leave the interviewer with a good feeling about the possibility of having you as an employee.

MAKING THE CALL

In Chapter 6 you learned the best time to make the call, so be sure to call at that time. If you don't make contact, try one of the alternative times, even calling within 15 minutes before or after business hours.

Because you know the secretary's name and have established rapport, you should have little problem getting through. Never assume, however.

"Mr. Lake's office."

"Good morning, this is Pete Springs. Is this Ms. Preston?" Note that you ask if this is Ms. Preston; you don't immediately ask for Mr. Lake. That shows her that you value her as a person. It also gives you the opportunity to check whether you are indeed speaking to Ms. Preston rather than someone else.

If the impression you have made on her so far has only been average, or if she is especially busy at the moment, she may say: "What can I do for you?"

If you have been a hit with her and she is not harried, she may say: "Yes it is, Mr. Springs. How are *you* today?"

In either case, respond to the question in a friendly way and ask: "Is this a good time to speak with Mr. Lake?"

Note that you don't just ask her to put him on the line. You ask for her opinion about whether Mr. Lake would be receptive to your call. Indirectly, you also show her that you appreciate and respect her help and judgment. Good secretaries are careful about such things, and they appreciate supervisors who have the savvy to know that.

If she says no, respect that and ask when it would be a good time to try to reach him. She may even suggest that she will have him call you and may even ask *you* when might be a good time. If she doesn't ask, give her a couple of options. "So that we use Mr. Lake's time well, he might try reaching me at either 10:30 or 2:30. How does that sound to you, Ms. Preston?"

When you and Mr. Lake do connect, you will have only about 30 seconds in which to establish the tone of the transaction. Respect Lake's time and get right to the point. Smile as you speak. It helps, even if you have to force it at first.

"Good morning, Mr. Lake. This is Pete Springs. I want to thank you for meeting with me the other day. Assuming that no decision has been made yet, do you have time for a couple of questions about the opening?"

His response may be that he is busy, but I have watched executives try to convey that impression even as they sipped a cup of coffee and read the morning paper. You are safe if you say that you understand and that you will be brief.

Now go directly to your first question. It should be an open-ended question, one that can't be answered with a simple yes or no. Make certain that whatever you ask will reflect favorably on you. It should be something that was not answered specifically during the interview but that may have gotten you thinking in greater depth.

Let's say, for example, you were told during the interview that the opening was created because they need someone to head an important project coming up in six months.

"Mr. Lake, I wonder if you could elaborate a bit on what the social responsibility project will involve in terms of publics identified and the timetable for implementation."

Here is what you have already accomplished even before you receive Lake's response: You've asked an intelligent question; you've shown an interest in something that is obviously important to him; and you've reminded him of one of your strengths.

It would be difficult to predict where the conversation might go from here, but pay close attention to whatever response Lake gives. The seeds of your follow-up questions are planted within the words he chooses. Listen "care-fully" and let that show in the way you follow up Lake's response with another question.

Don't try to keep the call going an unduly long time. In fact, even if Lake tries to extend it, you would be well advised to get off the phone rather quickly. There is a risk that staying on the line could engage you in a second interview, and it is never to your advantage to have it by phone. If Lake seems to be asking second-interview questions of you, suggest that you meet again.

"Mr. Lake, it sounds like we might want to discuss this further, but I want to respect your time this morning. Perhaps we should get together again. When would be a good time for us to do that?" Note the word choices. If you also took care to match his voice tones, you may be on your way to discussing another interview. If Lake isn't prepared to set that up, he'll say so. Possibly, he'll offer to get back to you. That's fine. Close the call with appreciation and say you'll look forward to speaking with him further.

If he is ready to go for the second meeting, either he will schedule it or he may put his secretary back on the line to make the appointment. If Ms. Preston comes on the line, work with her. She knows Lake's schedule. You need her to get you in there at the time that is right for him, not for you. That is how sales are made. Be sure to express your appreciation as you close the call, and let her know that you look forward to seeing her again.

Is this method of dealing with the secretary important? Ask a successful person in sales. Ask an acquaintance of mine who hadn't realized that his boss was about to be transferred and that he would inherit his boss's secretary.

Perhaps the best part of this "selling" approach is that you don't have to *sell* at all. You should simply have a sensitivity to the needs of others and a readiness to act accordingly. When seen that way, making your follow-up calls to prospects need not be stressful at all. In fact, with proper planning, a cold call can leave all the parties with a warm feeling.

22
Callbacks

I f you are interviewing for a managerial, professional, or supervisory position, the employer is unlikely to make you an offer on your first interview. In most cases, he or she will need to compare you with other candidates before making a decision. Your interviewer will most likely consider such factors as impressions made, credentials, salary ranges, experiences that relate specifically to the opening, and styles. Often, the final judgments may even be influenced by such unspoken criteria as how the people making the decision would feel about having a particular candidate as a boss, character witness, confidant, ally in time of need, or neighbor. For better or worse, that's human nature, that's life.

In most organizations, it is unlikely that any one individual, even the CEO, would be willing to make a unilateral decision. On the contrary, most executives will want to ensure that their colleagues feel comfortable with whatever decision is made. Thus, they may want to have others see you, talk with you, and get to know you better before a decision is made.

The Follow-up Interview

The follow-up interview simply means that you have survived the second cut. It does not mean you have the job locked up. Everything that pertained to your first interview will apply here as well. You will have to resist any urge to act as though you were already on board when you meet the follow-up interviewers. In fact, they could be especially sensitive to any attitude that even hints that you consider their interviews to be irrelevant.

Most likely, you will be called back for one visit in which you will meet one or more people who will have some input into which candidate is hired. Each person who interviews you will have a different orientation—his or her own way of determining what attributes are important in the candidate who is selected.

In many ways, when you return for follow-ups, you need to treat each individual's interview as though it were a brand-new situation and you were starting from scratch. For instance, you will need to get in step with each new person, so remember your skills for establishing rapport and practice them well. You may also be asked many of the same questions the first interviewer asked you. Be patient and don't let this annoy you. The follow-up interviewers are just trying to do their job. Help them succeed. They may have even less interviewing experience than your first interviewer had.

Your follow-up interviews may also give you more of an opportunity to see the organization at work and to get a flavor of things. Now that the pressure of the initial interview is off, you may have more time to observe whatever you missed the first time.

Just as the employer may be hoping to see you in a more natural light, so you should be looking for similar information. What *is* the receptionist like? How *does* the secretary treat you now? Has the first interviewer's personality or style changed this time? You, of course, shouldn't change, but the others you met might. Observe the nature of the changes. Have the others become more friendly? Relaxed? More assuming? Demanding? Are you treated with the same level of courtesy and respect?

How about the people you are meeting for the first time in this follow-up interview? They will be drawing heavily on what the first interviewer said about you, so notice their attitudes as well. Equally important, determine their role in the hiring process. Find out from what perspective your initial interviewer has sought their input. Knowing that can help you provide the kind of information that will guide them in making their recommendations. Beyond seeking their observations, your initial interviewer may have asked the others to meet with you to provide information. If so, it's important to know that as well.

Before you participate in the follow-up interviews, you should know who will be meeting with you—their titles, their responsibilities or functions, and which areas of expertise they might have been asked to comment on. In all likelihood, their questions will be both very general and very specific. Having gotten this far in the screening process, you may be halfway hired in their estimation. Thus, they may want to talk with you in a more conversational way than your first interviewer did. Unquestionably, they will want to know more about you as a person if they're going to be working with you, and many of their inquiries will be intended that way.

Make certain you are comfortable with anything you are about to disclose before you say a word. Rarely will an interviewer intentionally set you up to disclose something that might hurt your chances of getting the job, but it has happened. Just as risky, however, is the interviewer with whom you feel so comfortable that you decide to bare your soul. Doing so may feel good, but most candidates have told me that it cost them.

It also doesn't hurt to keep in mind that any one of the follow-up interviewers may not want to see you—or anyone else—hired for the post. It could be that they wanted the position or that one of their colleagues was passed over. It may be that they believe in promoting from within and don't like to see outsiders hired at your level. One never knows, so don't become complacent. Stay on your toes.

The job-related questions you are asked by follow-up interviewers will often reflect their specific areas of expertise. Thus, when the interviewers shift into those topics, they may become very specific, even to asking you about topics beyond your scope.

The rule here? As always, don't try to fake it. If you don't know, say so. In fact, it might be a good strategy to ask, rather than tell, when such questions arise. After all, if the interviewer is the expert, what better compliment could you find than to express an interest in his or her specific information or knowledge? In the process, you may learn more that will help you with your own decision.

If you did not meet people who would report to you or hold positions equal to yours during the first interview, you may have an opportunity to meet them now. Recognize that you have as much right to ask questions of people at those levels as they have to ask questions of you. Again, always know ahead of time with whom you will be speaking. As much as possible, make your questions appropriate to the individual.

How long have they held their positions? How would they describe their own functions? How do they see the department's mission? Where do they feel the organization is headed? What activities are they presently engaged in? What comments might they have about those projects?

As always, attitude is everything, so stay friendly with and interested in each person you meet. One candidate who did that successfully was able to draw an employee into disclosing a situation that would need her immediate attention once she was hired. Yet it had not been mentioned by the first interviewer and two subsequent ones.

WRAPPING UP THE FOLLOW-UP

When your follow-up interview draws to a close, you will most likely be returned to the person who invited you back. Most participants in my seminars have told me that the first question they have generally been asked upon their return is: "Well, how'd it go?"

Since follow-ups frequently involve meetings with several people, your interviewer may have been receiving feedback all along and may know more than you do about how things went. Nonetheless, you should focus on how *well* things went and have good things to say about the people you met and the information they shared with you. But don't be a Pollyanna. If you saw or heard things about the position that you would like clarified, this is the time to bring them up. To fail to do so now could leave you vulnerable once in the job.

Missing Information Somewhere during your interviews, you should have been able to learn about your office, your hours, your physical location, your secretary, the availability of a contract, benefits, policy on salary increases, moving expenses (if applicable), the community to which you would be moving, schools, activities, and more.

You should have also learned something about the drawbacks to the job; every position has them. Use this closing opportunity to ask about areas that the host feels could be improved within the company, the department, or the community. If you haven't gotten this information, ask for it. Any respectable employer will want you to have a fair, balanced picture upon which to make your decision.

Until now, we have placed a lot of emphasis on what could go wrong and what to watch out for. That does not mean you should expect the worst. On the contrary, most follow-up interviews are pleasant experiences, and you would need little coaching to get through them. However, this book has an obligation to help you prepare, and that means continuing to help you recognize where interview traps may lie and to show you how to deal with them successfully.

When you wrap up this meeting with your host interviewer, you may find that you still have not been offered a job. This too is not uncommon. Most such sessions close with a comment such as "We'll get back to you" from the interviewer. Stay poised. Here is one time when the sales approach to skills marketing must be modified. Don't press for the order. Instead, recall the trial closes I discussed earlier and try one of them. At best, you will learn a bit more about where you stand, but the host will undoubtedly want to talk with the others in depth before making a commitment.

Close the interview with all the finesse you used during the first meeting and be on your way. Immediately jot down your impressions, just as you did before. You will have to send a personal note to each person you met, so you must obtain either business cards from them or a list of names and titles from your host.

Keep your notes brief, and be sure each one includes a reference to something job-related that each individual discussed with you. Close by thanking each person for the time spent with you, but avoid the temptation to comment on "how wonderful it would be" to work with him or her.

The Final Step

Within a reasonable period, you should receive either a phone call or a letter from your host. If you are called, the likelihood is that you are being made an offer and there is some room for a modest amount of negotiation, perhaps on salary but more likely on other points such as a moving allowance and a starting date.

In this negotiation, don't quibble. Just assure your caller that you know you will be treated fairly. Stress that you will trust your employer's judgment. You will gain more from that approach than you would by arguing over nickels and dimes, and you will be more assured of being made an offer.

When the offer is made, ask for a few days to consider it. You need not explain why, even (and perhaps especially) if you are waiting for a better prospect to come through. Set a specific time limit that you can both agree on, and be sure to get back to the caller at that time.

If you receive a letter, it may also contain good news. The terms will be more fixed, however, even though the letter may extend an invitation to discuss terms further. It may be to your advantage to follow up a written offer with a phone call, since a letter frequently does not contain everything you may wish to know.

When You Decline an Offer

Perhaps, for whatever reason, you find it necessary to decline an offer. If so, you have no obligation to be brutally frank about your reasons. Just say that you have decided to continue to look elsewhere and that you appreciate the time and effort the host and the other interviewers expended on your behalf.

One seminar participant told me he once turned down a job because he didn't like the working conditions—dirty, unsafe, and so on. He tried giving the caller a courteous yet ambiguous turndown. The caller, with whom he had established a good rapport during the interview, responded by saying, "I don't blame you. I'm not going to be here much longer myself." Unprofessional, perhaps, but it certainly reinforced the candidate's decision.

When You're Turned Down

If you have been turned down, you will most likely learn about it by letter, since a letter is a safer way to convey that information. Whether the bad news comes by letter or by phone, don't take it personally. You must have scored well above the pack just to get as far as you did. You must have been liked, and the decision may have been a difficult one.

Let the caller know that, and express your appreciation for what the people you met must have gone through in making a final decision. You can be assured that they have done their best to select the person most likely to be successful on the job. Once again, what goes around comes around, and people in any given field tend to cross paths when they least expect it throughout their careers. A professional attitude now may hold you in good stead at another time. Although you may not like the "rejection," you will certainly be able to live with yourself a lot better if you remain the pro that you know you are.

When you accept an offer, always acknowledge it in writing and spell out conditions as you understand them. At this point you can also express your enthusiasm about working with the host and ask him or her to extend that feeling to the others whom you have met.

Soon you will be on the job.

23
Once You're Hired

Never go back to work.
Always go forward to work.
Back to work is what you
MUST do . . . forward to work
is what you WANT to do.
                    —Eric Butterworth

You may have gone through several interviews before being hired; people have told me of enduring as many as six. Once you accept the position, an employer will want to keep in contact with you and help you in any way possible. You may be sent copies of the organization's publications and anything else that will help you get to know your new employer better.

If you will have to move to take the new job, you may also be sent copies of the local newspaper, real estate magazines, county maps, and other relevant material, including, perhaps, a description of the area prepared by the local chamber of commerce. Some employers even pay for trips to find a suitable place to live. The employer will want to help you learn more about the community and its lifestyle so you can adapt comfortably.

Your First Day

Many executives have told me that during the first day in a new office, they felt myriad emotions unlike those aroused by most other experiences in life. Much of this can be accounted for by how the employer handles your welcome. Some may address the new manager's needs and ensure that the entry is a smooth one. Others may believe it's best to "leave the new manager alone" for the first day or two.

Because welcoming styles vary, new managers' reactions also vary. Some have said there is almost an "awesome sense of having left a part of you behind." Others have said they experienced a "hollow feeling," a "sense of emptiness," upon seeing their new, vacant office. Still others have reported a sense of welcome from the start. Again, it depends mostly upon the new employee's supervisor.

When You Arrive

Unless you are keenly aware of office protocol before you move in, leave your personal belongings and your nest-building needs at home for a few days. People will be watching, and some will be checking to see whether you do anything out of the ordinary.

For example, some organizations have a distinct hierarchy of office appurtenances, even though their executives have disclaimed any knowledge of it until I pointed it out to them. Take an innocuous example, the stapler. At one level, it may be battleship gray. At the next level, black. At another level, it may have a walnut-grained plastic insert. At yet another level, it may have a solid chip of walnut screwed to the top. All are symbols of station, regardless of what their users may say. Or how about a simple pencil holder? Possibilities might include an old cup, a plastic holder, a metal holder, a wood-and-brass holder, or yes, even a gold-filigreed holder matching the rest of the items on the desk.

Anything you move into the office, anything you change, will be noticed by someone. People do indeed attach meanings to such things, just as men and women in the military do to the number of stripes on sleeves or the design and metal used for brass on shoulders.

No Fish, Please An executive who went through one of my seminars reported that he took an aquarium—tropical fish, stand, and all—into his office the first day. Three days later he was moved to another office and had to get special help to move the fish tank. Two weeks later he was moved again, and this time he had to move his own fish. When he was moved again after another month, he took the aquarium home. He stayed in the same office for three years.

He was never told directly to get rid of the fish, and he was still not certain the fish had anything to do with his moves. But he did receive

numerous comments and some friendly gibes about his fish each time
he had to move them. The message? It's almost as important to fit in
during that first week as it is to contribute to the tasks for which you
were hired.

Typical First Day

Most first days on the job will go something like this: You will arrive
at your boss's office at least 10 minutes before the start of business. You
will be dressed and groomed appropriately, briefcase in hand, and with
whatever tools of the trade you feel might be important to have with
you.

You may chat briefly with the secretary and then visit with your
new boss. At that time, he or she should outline the day for you.
Perhaps you will be briefed in more detail about the job. Perhaps you
will need to process forms. You may also be taken to the personnel
department for further briefing and orientation. Either before this or
afterward you may be given the opportunity to visit with your staff or
your superiors.

Arranging for Feedback

If you haven't already learned what your employer ranks as highest in
priority for you in filling the post, this is a good time to find out. Try
to do this as quickly as possible, because it's your insurance that you
will get off to a successful start in your boss's eyes.

You should also ask for your own copy of departmental policies and
procedures, organization chart, and job descriptions. Ask about regularly
held meetings, who calls them, who attends, who sets the agenda, and
so on. Find out where you are expected to eat on a regular basis and
with whom.

Obtain an agenda for the projects that are expected of you. At the
same time, ask to set target dates for preliminary evaluations rather
than wait for formally scheduled reviews. Invite your boss to brief
you on each person who reports to you. He or she may not have
been able to go into detail about them before you were hired, but you
will need to know now. Ask what functions each one performs and

find out about any duties that the person may have assumed or may be carrying out that are not shown in the job description or on the organization chart.

You can also ask about the availability of supplies, equipment, and even furniture if you need it. Again, a note of caution: Go for the highest-ranking symbols your boss will let you have, but don't select anything that is parallel to, or above, whatever he or she has.

If you have a private secretary, arrange to meet him or her—before you meet your staff, if possible. To insure your mutual survival, your secretary may be willing and able to fill you in on things your boss may not have mentioned. Be careful here, too, however. Your secretary may still harbor a loyalty to someone who was moved into a higher position or is now your equal in another function. As a result, the secretary could be a conduit directly to this person. Such a situation could work to your advantage or to your detriment.

Stress loyalty—your secretary's to you—right from the start. A secretary whose former boss was fired may welcome you or may resent you. Be cautious until you find out which. If you felt that you were the knight in shining armor when you strode confidently into the building, you may now begin to wonder if you are perceived by some to be the enemy. Neither is likely to be totally true. For some, you may be the answer to a dream; for others, you may be a nightmare of historic proportions. Most will regard you as neutral until the game begins in earnest and the chips begin to stack up in front of the players.

Visiting with Staff

When it comes time to visit with members of your department, whether your staff or your superiors, everyone will want to check you out. This may not be done as blatantly as a pack of dogs eye a newcomer, but it has some of the same overtones. They will want to know where you've been, what you've been doing, whom you've done it with, and more. And all the while, they will try to determine whether to accept you, where you might fit in the hierarchy (often despite what the organizational chart says), and how they should relate to you.

In the days and weeks to come, they will check you out even further. Some will ally with you; others may try to test you; and one or two may even try to challenge you. Now, we can put as genteel a face as we like on all this, but it comes down to the same issue: Will you be accepted or will you not? There must be some significance behind the phrase, "It's a dog-eat-dog world," that we hear so often.

How you handle this will be a matter of your own personal style as much as anything else, and strategies for successful survival on the job go well beyond the scope of this book. As we said earlier, however, first impressions can carry forward with you, so make certain they're the ones that will serve you best.

Can You Succeed?

When I discussed the Yeager Performance Model, you learned that the three essential ingredients for success depend upon whether the individual

1. Wants to succeed (desire)
2. Knows how to succeed (knowledge of people and requisite skills)
3. Has the chance to succeed (opportunity)

In hiring you, the employer determined that you had the credentials and the desire, but only he or she knew whether the position carried with it the opportunity for you to be successful on the job. When you asked your questions about reporting relationships and responsibilities, and when you met members of your staff in advance (if that opportunity was extended to you when you requested it), you learned as much as a candidate could about whether the job was set up so that you could succeed. Now it will be up to you to check into all that even further.

If at any point you find you are being held accountable for something but lack the authority to get it done, speak to your boss at once. Don't pass it off in the hope it will go away. You are a member of your boss's team now, so you should work to keep his or her support. Seek advice, guidance, direction, involvement. With tact, do whatever you feel you must do to ensure that you can deliver what you have been hired to do. Remember, nothing can ever be the way it may have seemed while you were on the outside looking in.

If you experience difficulties, you have an obligation to yourself and your supervisor to report that in the most fair and accurate way you can. Since you are still new, it will most likely be inappropriate for you to recommend solutions, but you can certainly elicit them, listen carefully, and act appropriately.

If you feel that your supervisor's own actions or inactions are contributing to the problem, you will have to tread carefully, of course.

More than one recent hire has been terminated rather quickly for going over a boss's head or attempting an end run. Even if you go to the personnel department, whatever you say is likely to bounce back. After all, you are still the outsider, and the pack regards its survival as paramount.

Not every job is going to be perfect, and not every situation is going to require the boss's involvement. Be judicious in calling him or her in to help you with a situation. Some situations may resolve themselves in time, but you will have to be astute in determining which ones.

Get the Word Out

Now that you are on the job, be sure to notify potential employers who still have you under consideration. Phone calls are appropriate, but follow up with brief letters so you increase the impact. The recipients will appreciate the courtesy and respect you even more. Perhaps one day you may be in touch with them again.

You should also contact everyone who has helped you throughout your search—*everyone.* That includes the people you interviewed for information, librarians, and anyone else who may have extended you a special favor. Again, a phone call followed by a brief note would be appropriate—and appreciated. People tend to remember favorably those who were considerate to them.

Build Your Résumé

Now that you are in the job, consider how difficult it probably was to document your accomplishments or relationships when a potential employer asked you for information to support your statements. Never allow yourself to be caught short again.

From this day forward, write memos, notes to file, detailed reports. Send the originals to the right people, the ones from whose names you'll benefit most as documentation if you need to reference these projects in future interviews. Keep copies of any commendation letters, memos, or anything else that shows that you made a contribution to a specific project. If you are entitled to copies of your performance evaluations, keep them as well.

Finally, store this material in a secure file *at home.* Horror stories of leaders who have staged midnight raids on their own managers aside, you never know when you'll be glad you have this material where no one else can see or touch it.

Although these are good procedures to follow in any career, you should be especially prudent about maintaining such information if you are in a high-turnover field. The track record you claim on your résumé and in your interviews will have far more meaning if you can document it.

Epilogue

I have tried to paint a realistic picture in these pages, and what happens to you in your new job will depend largely upon factors that are often not of your own choosing, making, or liking. The good news, and the bad news, is that this country's organizations are changing. As they change, employment turnover is increasing. A 1988 report by the Bureau of Labor Statistics estimates that the average graduate of a 4-year college can now expect to hold more than ten jobs over his or her career.

Consider the departures as potential openings for which you may well qualify. Although a number of departures may result from mergers, downsizings, bankruptcies, and the like, somebody is going to have to do the job. Increasingly, our business society is making it more attractive for organizations to retain specialized consultants rather than maintain permanent staffs to perform the same functions. Consider that as another area in which you may be successful.

Finally, it may take you longer than you anticipated to find the right job, but if you follow the marketing approach presented in this book and then follow through with the sales techniques provided, you will succeed.

Here's to your success!

Reading List

I hope this book has helped you develop a marketing plan that will help you get hired as it has helped others. However, no single book can address the special situations and needs of every reader. So, read everything that interests you on this subject. The reading list that follows provides a starting point; it contains the references that my seminar participants and private clients mention most often.

To make certain you find all the information you need, look in your libary's reference directories for books and recently published articles on any aspect of this topic that interests you. Be willing to explore any avenues that might lead to information that can help you.

There are well over a hundred books in print on the interview process alone—many of which are written to help guide the people who will be interviewing you. Read these and you could gain more insight into how skilled employers approach an interview. You may also want to read books and current articles on how to open and close sales, since selling is an essential part of what you will be doing.

The references that follow merely suggest a start, a way to begin finding the information you will need to market your employment skills successfully. As you look at each book, examine its bibliography and then pursue the titles that appeal to you. Your librarian may be able to help you.

Periodical Indexes

Business Periodicals Index. New York: H.W. Wilson.
Directory of Corporate Affiliations (Who Owns Whom). New York: National Register Publishing Company.
Directory of Directories. Detroit: Gale's Research Company.

Encyclopedia of Associations. Detroit: Gale's Research Company.
Million Dollar Directory. Parsippany, NJ: Dun's Marketing Services.
National Directory of State Agencies. Bethesda, MD: National Standards Association.
Reference Book of Corporate Managements. Parsippany, NJ: Dun's Marketing Services.
Standard & Poor's Industry Surveys. New York: Standard & Poor's.
Standard & Poor's Register of Corporations, Directors and Executives. New York: Standard & Poor's.
Thomas' Register of American Manufacturers. New York: Thomas.
U.S. Industrial Outlook. Washington: U.S. Department of Commerce/International Trade Administration.
Ward's Business Directory. Belmont, CA: Information Access Company.

Books

Allen, Jeffrey G., and Jess Gorkin. *Finding the Right Job at Midlife.* New York: Simon & Schuster, 1985.
Bird, Caroline. *Everything a Woman Needs to Know to Get Paid What She's Worth.* New York: David McKay, 1973.
Boll, Carl R. *Executive Jobs Unlimited.* Toronto: Macmillan, 1965.
Bolles, Richard N. *What Color Is Your Parachute?* Berkeley, CA: Ten Speed Press, 1987.
Bolton, Robert. *People Skills.* Englewood Cliffs, NJ: Prentice-Hall, 1979.
Bramson, Robert M. *Coping with Difficult People.* New York: Ballantine, 1981.
Conklin, Robert. *How to Get People to Do Things.* New York: Ballantine, 1979.
Cole, Diane. *Hunting the Headhunters: A Woman's Guide.* New York: Simon & Schuster, 1988.
Drake, John. *Interviewing for Managers.* New York: American Management Association, 1972.
Fisher, Roger, and William Ury. *Getting to Yes.* New York: Penguin, 1981.
Hill, Napoleon, and W. Clement Stone. *Success Through a Positive Mental Attitude.* New York: Pocket Books, 1977.
Irish, Richard K. *Go Hire Yourself an Employer.* Garden City, NY: Anchor, 1973.
Johnson, Barbara L. *Working Wherever You Want.* Englewood Cliffs, NJ: Prentice-Hall, 1983.
Jones, Charles T. *Life Is Tremendous.* Harrisburg, PA: Executive Books, 1968.
Keefe, William F. *Open Minds: The Forgotten Side of Communication.* New York: AMACOM, 1975.
Korda, Michael. *Success.* New York: Ballantine, 1978.
LaHaye, Timothy. *Your Temperament: Discover its Potential.* Wheaton, IL: Tyndale, 1984.

Lee, Patricia. *The Complete Guide to Job Sharing.* New York: Walker & Co., 1983.

Mackay, Harvey. *Swim with the Sharks.* New York: Morrow, 1988.

Mann, Stanley. *Triggers: A New Approach to Self-Motivation.* Englewood Cliffs, NJ: Prentice-Hall, 1987.

Martel, Myles. *Mastering the Art of Q & A.* Homewood, IL: Dow Jones–Irwin, 1989.

McDowell, Josh. *Building Your Self-Image.* Wheaton, IL: Living Books, 1986.

McGinnis, Alan Loy. *Confidence: How to Succeed at Being Yourself.* Minneapolis: Augsburg, 1987.

Neuhauser, Peg C. *Tribal Warfare in Organizations.* Cambridge, MA: Ballinger, 1988.

Nierenberg, Gerald I. *The Art of Negotiating.* New York: Pocket Books, 1981.

Phillips, Gerald M. *Help for Shy People.* Englewood Cliffs, NJ: Prentice-Hall, 1981.

Qubein, Nido R. *Get the Best from Yourself.* Englewood Cliffs, NJ: Prentice-Hall, 1983.

Rafe, Stephen C. *How to Be Prepared to Think on Your Feet.* New York: Harper Business, 1990.

Robertson, Jason. *How to Win in a Job Interview.* Englewood Cliffs, NJ: Prentice-Hall, 1978.

Rodgers, Buck, and Irv Levey. *Getting the Best . . . Out of Yourself and Others.* New York: Harper & Row, 1987.

Schwartz, David J. *The Magic of Thinking Big.* N. Hollywood, CA: Wilshire, 1959.

Stoop, David. *Self Talk: Key to Personal Growth.* Old Tappan, NJ: Revell, 1982.

Uris, Auren, and Jack Tarrant. *How to Keep from Getting Fired.* Chicago: Henry Regnery, 1975.

Viscott, David S. *How to Make Winning Your Lifestyle.* New York: Dell, 1972.

Yate, Martin J. *Knock 'Em Dead—with Great Answers to Tough Interview Questions.* Holbrook, MA: Bob Adams, 1987.

Yeager, Joseph. *Thinking About Thinking with NLP.* Cupertino, CA: Meta Publications, 1985.

Zunin, Leonard, and Natalie Zunin. *Contact: The First Four Minutes.* New York: Ballantine, 1972.

Additional Resources

Outpatient Counseling: John D. Brenner, Ph.D., President, John D. Brenner Associates, Inc. 14 Williamsburg North, Colts Neck, NJ, 07722.

Index

abilities, interview questions concerning, 140, 152
accessories, 93
accomplishments, 4
accusations, 147
achievements: documentation of, 207–208; emphasizing correct, 51; needs for, 6, 7; résumé based on, 36, 39–41, 51
action words, 55–56
advertising, self-, 65; *see also* help wanted ads
affiliation needs, 6, 7
age: of applicant, 46; of employer, 70
agencies: *see* employment agencies
alcohol, 95, 171
allergies, 95
appearance, 91–95; clothing, 91–93; grooming, 94–95; tips for, 94
application forms, 119; completion of, 62, 114
appointments: rescheduling interviews, 115, 171–172; second interview, 195; telephone, 78–80; telephone techniques for scheduling, 76–80, 193–195

appreciation, expressing, 110, 112, 178–179, 200, 201, 207
Approach I communication style, 11–12, 125, 128
Approach II communication style, 11–12, 122–123, 125, 128
aptitude: analysis of, 18; tests of, 173
assessment, personal, 18, 22–23
assumption, 146
attitude: in follow-up process, 75–79; of interviewer, 89, 119–125, 131, 133–135, 182, 183; of job candidate, 87–91, 98–99, 145–146, 178, 183, 193
auditory mode, 81, 82, 129, 160, 161, 177
Avoidance I communication style, 11–12, 122–124, 125, 128
Avoidance II communication style, 11–12, 125, 128

B

baiting, 147
balance sheet, personal, 16, 21

Benson, Herbert, 90
biography, personal, 53
Birdwhistell, Ray T., 126
blind ads, 63–64
body language, 101, 126–129,
  131–132; assigning meanings to,
  126–127; in employment
  interview, 110; exercises in
  reading, 125–129; gestures in,
  127, 128, 132; as outward
  expression, 127; posture, 127,
  128, 132, 169; standard signals
  in, 127
bridging, 129–130, 160–161
Business Periodicals Index,
  69

C

career changes, 49–50; education
  and, 49–50; résumé format and,
  38–41, 44–45, 49–50
career counseling services, 65
career goals, 130
chronological résumé, 34–38
church activities, 174
Civil Rights Act of 1964, Title VII
  of, 173–175
civil service examinations, 173
closing, interview, 176–179, 200
clothing, 91–93
college education, 46, 50
color, of business clothing, 92
committee projects, 51
communication style: auditory
  mode, 81, 82, 129, 160, 161,
  177; of interviewer, 11–13,
  122–125, 128; Rafe Model for
  analyzing, 11–13, 122–128; tactile
  mode, 81, 82, 129, 160, 161, 177;
  visual mode, 81, 82, 129, 160,
  161, 177

community service activities:
  evaluation of experiences in, 15,
  20
company information, 29–31, 68–71,
  89, 211–212
composite résumé, 38–41, 44–45
computers: list house information
  and, 68–70; in organization of
  direct-marketing campaign,
  71–73; use of, in job search, 70
consultants: advertising done by,
  65; job-hunting techniques of, 59
cover letters, 53–57; list of action
  words for, 55–56
credentials, 46, 50, 184, 185
credit for work done, 51
criminal record, 174

D

Dale, Edgar, 129
"Dale's Cone of Experience,"
  129
data bases, 69
degrees, college, 46, 50
delays, 114–115
diction, 96
difficult questions, 145, 156–158
direct-marketing campaign:
  follow-up in, 75–79; organization
  of system for, 71–73; standard
  letter for, 71, 73–74; *see also* job
  leads
direct-marketing letter, 71, 73–74;
  follow-up for, 75–79; list of
  action words for, 55–56; purpose
  of, 74
directories, 68–71; list of, 211–212;
  overview of, 29–31
Directory of Directories, 29, 69
disagreement, 155–156, 158–160
discrimination, 173–175

documentation of achievements,
207–208
dress code, corporate, 91–93

E

education: career change and,
49–50; evaluation of experiences
in, 15, 20; interview questions
concerning, 141–142, 153; lack of
degree, 46; in résumé, 46, 50; in
skills inventory, 17; special
situations and, 46, 50
embedment, 159
emotions: choice and, 131;
employment interview and,
90–91; *see also* personality tests;
stress
employers, current: references
from, 47–49; telephone calls from
potential employers and, 79–83
employers, past: employment
record and work history, 15–16,
19, 20, 46; references from,
47–49
employers, potential: analyzing,
27–33; follow-up telephone calls
to, 75–79; information sources
on, 29–33, 68–71, 89, 211–212;
large vs. small, 28; notification of
new job, 207; problems with
recruitment and hiring system,
58–60; telephone calls from,
79–83; *see also* employment
interviews; job leads; questions
asked by potential employer
employment agencies, 59; job leads
from, 61–62; references and, 47;
résumé circulation by, 47
employment interviews: appearance
and, 91–95; applicant's reactions
to, 180–185; arrival stage of,
111–115; attitude of job
candidate, 87–91, 98–99,
145–146, 178, 183, 193; avoiding
misunderstandings in, 162–166;
body language in, 110; checklist
for, 102; concluding stage of,
176–179; difficult questions in,
145, 156–158; disagreement and,
155–156, 158–160; establishing
rapport in, 105–108, 126–132,
160–161; evaluation by
interviewers in, 98; group, 98,
118, 167–171; illegal questions in,
137, 139, 173–175; information
about company in, 89;
information interviews and,
32–33, 60–61; initial contacts for,
32–33; interruption of, 171–172;
introductory stages of, 104–106,
111–115, 119–132; length of,
107, 108; listening in, 164–166;
luncheon, 171; narrative,
135–136; no-hire decisions and,
183–185; open-ended, 135;
personal expectations and, 6–10;
physical environment of, 107,
116–118, 168; preparing for,
87–103; purpose of, 133;
rehearsing for, 98–101, 163;
rescheduling, 115, 171–172; rest
before, 96–97; role-playing for,
101; scheduling, 76–80, 115,
171–172, 195; second, 183, 195,
196–200; stages of, 104–110;
standard question and answer,
136; stress, 133–135; telephone,
76, 83, 195; test-taking and,
172–173; timing of, 101–103;
types of, 133–136; types of
interviewers in, 97–98; voice and,
95–96, 101; waiting for, 114–115;
see also follow-up, post-interview;

interviewer; *entries beginning with* questions

employment record, 15–16, 19, 20, 46

enthusiam: of interviewer, 89; of job candidate, 106, 109

environmental assessment, 107, 114; of furniture arrangements, 116–118, 168; of interviewer's office, 107, 116–118; of reception area, 111–113

equal employment opportunity, 173–175

errors of fact, 146

expectations, analysis of, 6–10

experience: employment record and, 15–16, 19, 20, 46; evaluation of past, 15–16, 20; interview questions concerning, 140–141, 152; skills inventory and, 14–18

experts, information interviews with, 31–33

external satisfaction, 6, 7

eye contact, 120, 169

F

fabrics, 91, 92

Fanning, Patrick, 90

feedback: on first day of job, 204–205; on voice quality, 82

finances, personal: interview questions concerning, 141, 152–153

first day on job, 202–208; arrival and, 203–204; building résumé, 207–208; feedback and, 204–205; likelihood of success and, 206–207; notifying potential employers and, 207; staff visits during, 205–206; typical, 204

first impressions, 119, 126, 185, 206

fitting in, 185, 203–204

follow-up, direct marketing, 75–79; scheduling interviews in, 76; telephone, 75–79; timing of, 75–76

follow-up, post-interview, 10, 189–201: callbacks and, 183, 195, 196–200; job offers and, 200–201; letters in, 189–191, 193; perseverance and, 191–195; second interviews, 183, 195, 196–200; telephone calls in, 192–195; travel expenses and, 190–191, 192; wrapping up, 199–200

food: before interview, 95; luncheon interviews, 171; new job and, 204

footnotes, résumé, 46

forced choice questions, 147

Forty Plus, 64–65

freelance work, 51

friends: feedback on voice quality, 82; job leads from, 60–61; as job references, 48

functional résumé, 36–38, 41–47

furniture: environmental assessment and, 116–118; group interviews and, 168; in new office, 205

future pacing, 151, 159

G

Gale's Encyclopedia of Associations, 69

Gale's Encyclopedia of Business Information Sources, 69

gaps in career: for travel, 50–51; unemployment and, 51

gestures, 127, 128, 132
giving "permission," 160
goodbyes, 176–179
graduate degrees, 50
grooming, 94–95
group interviews, 98, 118, 167–171;
business stage of, 169–170; host
of, 168–169; reporting
relationships and, 167–170;
staying focused in, 170–171
Guide to American Directories, 69

H

hair, 94
hands, position of, 132
handshake, 93, 120
headhunters, 62
help wanted ads: problems of using,
59, 68; responding to, 63–64;
writing the ideal, 23–25
hobbies: evaluation of experiences
in, 15, 20; interview questions
concerning, 142, 144, 153
honesty, 139, 158, 198, 201
human resources department head,
97
hypothetical questions, 146–147

I

ideal job, 23–25
Industrial Arts Index, 29
industry: composite résumé format
for changing fields, 38–41, 44–45;
information interviews on, 31–33,
60–61; library information on,
29–33, 68–71, 89, 211–212
information interviews, 31–33,
60–61
interests, interview questions
concerning, 142, 144, 153

internal satisfaction, 6, 7
interruptions, of interview, 171–
172
interviewer: asking about decision
not to hire, 183–185; attitude of,
89, 119–125, 131, 133–135, 182,
183; avoiding misunderstandings
with, 162–166; body language
and, 126–129; in business stage
of interview, 106–108, 169, 170;
communication style of, 11–13,
123–125, 128; in conclusion stage
of interview, 109–110;
disagreement and, 155–156,
158–160; discomfort of, 88, 89,
105, 113–114, 116, 133–136;
establishing rapport with,
105–108, 126–132, 160–161;
evaluation techniques of, 98, 185;
focusing energy on, 88, 89;
furniture arrangement and,
116–118, 168; group, 98, 118,
167–171; information sought by,
98; in introductory stage of
interview, 104–106, 111–115,
119–132; job applicant's analysis
of, 182; matching speech patterns
of, 129–130, 160–161, 177; office
of, 107, 116–118; personality of,
11, 107, 121–125, 128; roles
played by, 155; tone of interview
and, 105–106; types of, 97–98;
see also employment interviews;
questions asked by potential
employer
interviews: business stage of,
106–108, 169–170; conclusion
stage of, 109–110; information,
31–33, 60–61; introductory stage
of, 104–106, 111–115, 119–132;
parts of, 104–110; personality of
interviewer and, 11, 107,

121–125, 128; types of, 133–136;
see also employment interviews
introductory stage of employment
interview, 104–106, 111–115,
119–132
invoices, for travel expense
reimbursement, 190–191,
192

J

jewelry, 93
job description, 204: interview
questions concerning, 140, 149,
151–152; writing the ideal, 23–25
job leads, 60–71; career counseling
services and, 65; data bases and,
69; from direct marketing, 65;
from employment agencies,
61–62; from help wanted
advertisements, 59, 63–64, 68;
information sources for locating,
29–33, 67–71, 89, 211–212; list
houses and, 68–70; from personal
contacts, 60–61; from placing
advertisements, 65; prospect
information and, 67; from search
firms, 62; from special help
groups, 64–65; system for
organization of, 71–73; through
professional associations, 62
job offers, 176: accepting, 200, 201;
declining, 201; failure to receive,
183–185, 201; negotiation and,
200; reasons for not receiving,
183–185, 201

K

kinesthetic (tactile) mode, 81, 82,
129, 160, 161, 177
Korda, Michael, 116, 117

L

labeling, 138
LaHaye Temperament Analysis,
10–11
leading question, 147
leads: *see* job leads
letters: to accept job offers, 200,
201; cover, 53–57; direct
marketing, 55–56, 71, 73–79;
post-interview follow-up,
189–191, 193, 200; to potential
employers on acceptance of job
offer, 207; turndown, 201
linking, 160
listening, 157, 170; in employment
interviews, 164–166
list houses, 68–70
luncheon interviews, 171

M

McKay, Matthew, 90
makeup, 94, 95
management: *see* people skills
matching technique, 129–130,
160–161, 177; in telephone calls,
81–82
meals: *see* food
medications, 95
Mehrabian, Albert T., 130
memory, 129, 130, 160, 165
men: business clothing of, 91–93;
grooming and, 94–95
military: evaluation of experiences
in, 15, 20
Miller's Law of Seven, 130
Million Dollar Directory, 29
misunderstanding, avoiding,
162–166; listening and, 164–165;
miscommunication and, 162–163;

options in, 165–166; rehearsals and, 163

motivation: personal sources of, 4–6, 7; Yeager Performance Model for analyzing, 7–10, 206

multiple-part questions, 147

Myers-Briggs personality inventory, 10

N

names: correct pronunciation of, 77; correct spelling of, 77; group interviews and, 167–168; of people no longer at company, 77; of secretaries, 112, 193

narrative interview, 135–136

needling, 146

needs, analysis of personal, 4–6, 7

negotiation, 200

new job: *see* first day on job; job offer

nonverbal messages: *see* body language

note-taking: in group interviews, 170; post-interview, 180–183, 193, 200; on prospects cards, 71–73, 83

O

offering statement, 34–35, 41

offers, job: *see* job offers

office, 114; analysis of potential employer's, 181; furniture arrangement in, 107, 116–118, 168; of interviewer, 107, 116–118, 168; moving into new, 203–204

open-ended interview, 135

opinions: of interviewer, 182;

interview questions concerning, 137–138, 151

organization chart, 181, 204

P

pace, speaking, 96

part-time employment, 51

people skills: external focus and, 6, 11–13; internal focus and, 6, 11–13; personal assessment of, 18, 22–23

perseverance, 191–195

personality: body language and, 128; of employer, 71; of interviewer, 107, 121–125, 128; interview questions concerning, 138–139, 142–144, 151, 153; résumé and, 53

personality tests, 10–13, 172–173; LaHaye Temperament Analysis, 10–11; Myers-Briggs, 10; Rafe Model, 11–13, 122–128

personnel department, 97, 204, 207

photographs, with résumé, 52

placement services: of employment agencies, 47, 59, 61–62; of professional associations, 62; of search firms, 62

policies and procedures, 204

posture, 127, 128, 132, 169

power: furniture arrangements and, 116–118; of job candidate, 118; listening and, 164; needs for, 6, 7; of secretaries, 112

Power (Korda), 116, 117

priorities, establishment of, in new job, 204–205

probing questions, 150–154, 162–163, 165–166, 170, 174

professional associations, as source of job leads, 62

progressive relaxation, 97
prospects cards, 71–73, 83
psychological tests, 173
published works, 50

Q

questions asked by job candidate,
89, 108, 148–154; follow-up,
193–195; group interviews and,
167, 169–170; list of sample, 149,
151–153; in post-interview
analysis, 180–183; probing,
150–154, 162–163, 165–166, 170,
174; reasons for not being hired,
183–185; in rehearsal for
employment interview, 99; in
screening calls, 83; in second
interviews, 198–199
questions asked by potential
employer, 108, 137–147;
concerning factual background,
137; concerning opinions and
viewpoints, 137–138, 151;
concerning temperatment or
personality, 138–139, 142–144,
151, 153; difficult, 145, 156–158;
legality of, 137, 139, 173–175;
list of sample, 139–144; in
screening calls, 83; stressful,
133–135; techniques used with,
146–147; types of, 135, 145–146;
see also employers, potential

R

Rafe Model of communication
styles, 11–13; Approach I
communication style, 11–12, 125,
128; Approach II communication
style, 11–12, 122–123, 125, 128;
Avoidance I communication style,
11–12, 122–124, 125, 128;
Avoidance II communication
style, 11–12, 125, 128
range, speaking, 96
rapport: skills for building, 105–108,
129–132, 160–161, 177; on the
telephone, 81–82
*Reader's Guide to Periodical
Literature,* 29, 70–71
reception room: introduction in,
112–113; observation of, 111–
113
record-keeping: in direct-marketing
campaign, 71; follow-up and, 207;
setting up system for, 71–73
references, 46–49; best types of,
48–49; checking, 48–49;
questionable, 47, 48; résumé and,
46–49, 52–53; seeking, 48–49
reframing, 159–160
rehearsal, for employment
interviews, 98–101, 163
reinterpretation, 146
relatives: job leads from, 60–61; as
job references, 48
Relaxation Response, The (Benson),
90
relaxation techniques, 90–91,
113–114; progressive relaxation,
97; rest as, 96–97
remembering, 129, 130, 160, 165
reporting relationships, 204–205;
analysis of, 181; group interviews
and, 167–170
rest, before employment
interviews, 96–97
restrooms, 113, 114
résumé, 34–57; achievements, 36,
39–41, 51; action words for,
55–56; avoiding use of, 53;
building, 207–208; career changes
and, 38–41, 44–45, 49–50;

chronological, 34–38; composite, 38–41, 44–45; controlling circulation of, 47; cover letter for, 53–57; development of, after accepting job offer, 207–208; employment agencies and, 47, 62; functional, 36–38, 41–47; help wanted ads and, 63–64; information interviews and, 32–33; offering statement and, 34–35, 41; purpose of, 51–52, 185; references and, 46–49, 52–53; special situations and, 49–51; stress interviews and, 133–135; tips for preparing, 52–53; use of, with application forms, 114

retirement speech, 25–26; offering statement and, 35

role-playing, for employment interviews, 101

S

salary: help wanted ads and, 63–64; interview questions concerning, 141, 152

satisfaction, internal vs. external, 6, 7

screening: group interviews and, 167, 168; telephone and, 83

search firms, 62

second interviews, 183, 195, 196–200

secretaries: getting past, 77, 193–195; importance of, 112; meeting your personal, 205; names of, 112, 193; phone appointments and, 78; relationship with, 193–195; thanking, 110, 112, 178–179; timing of telephone calls and, 76

self-advertising, 65

self-analysis, 3–26; of accomplishments, 4; in analysis of potential employers, 28–29; evaluation of past experience in, 15, 16, 20; of expectations for work, 6–10; ideal job and, 23–25; personal assessment in, 18, 22–23; personal balance sheet in, 16, 21; personality tests in, 10–13, 122–128, 172–173; of personal needs, 4–6, 7; of positive aspects of work, 4–6, 7; retirement speech and, 25–26, 35; skills and experience inventory in, 14–19; of strengths, 4, 5

self-consciousness, 88

Self-Esteem (McKay and Fanning), 90

skills and experience inventory, 14–19

skills tests, 172–173

sleep, before employment interviews, 96–97

smiling, 120–121

smoking, 96, 182

special help groups, 64–65

staff, meeting new, 205–206

Standard & Poors, 29

standard question & answer interview, 136

Standard Rate & Data Business Publications Directory, 69

static, in speech, 96

Statistics Sources, 69

strengths: analysis of, 4; list of potential, 5

stress: emotions and, 90–91; employment interviews and, 88–91, 107; environmental assessment and, 107;

fight-or-flight reaction to,
145–146; pre-interview, 113–114;
voice and, 95
stress interview, 133–135
success, 7–10, 206–207
suits, 92, 94
supervisor, as interviewer,
97–98
supplies, 205

T

tactile mode, 81, 82, 129, 160, 161,
177
tape recorders: rehearsal of
employment interview, 99;
telephone calls and, 82
team projects, 51
telephone appointments, 78–80
telephone calls: employment
interviews as, 76, 83, 195;
establishing rapport in, 81–82;
follow-up, to potential employers,
75–79; phone appointments and,
78–80; in post-interview
follow-up, 192–195; from
potential employers, 79–83; to
potential employers on
acceptance of job offer, 207;
procedures for completing,
77–79; recording, 82; scheduling
appointments and, 76–80;
193–195; screening, 83; timing
of, 76
temperament, analysis of, 10–13
termination, reasons for, 47
tests, 172–173; personality,
10–13, 172–173; skills,
172–173
therapy groups, 64–65
*Thomas' Register of American
Manufacturers,* 29, 69

timing: of employment interviews,
101–103; of follow-up to
direct-marketing letter, 75–76; of
initial contact with company, 70
Title VII, of Civil Rights Act of
1964, 173–175
titles, 197–198; group interviews
and, 167–168; in letters, 77; in
résumé, 36
travel: career gaps due to, 50–51;
expenses of, 178, 190–191, 192
trial closes, 177, 200
typesetting: of biography, 53; of
résumé, 52
typographical errors, 119

U

unemployment: career gaps and,
51; special help groups and,
64–65

V

verbal redirects: *see* probing
questions
videotaping, of rehearsals of
employment interview, 101
viewpoints: of interviewer, 182;
interview questions concerning,
137–138, 151
visualization: as a relaxation
technique, 90–91, 113–114; of
employment interview, 98–99
visual mode, 81, 82, 129, 160, 161,
177
voice tones: in employment
interview, 95–96, 101, 110, 121;
matching interviewer, 129–130,
160–161; on the telephone,
82
volume, speaking, 96

W

want ads: *see* help wanted ads
Who's Who, 29
women: business clothing of,
91–93; grooming and, 94–95;
illegal questions and, 174; return
of, to workforce, 49

work experience: *see* experience
worst-least questions, 145

Y

Yeager, Joseph P., 7–10
Yeager Performance Model, 7–10,
206

Rapport Communications prepares people at all levels in all fields to present information and respond to questions. Our methods help people make their points, achieve win-win outcomes, and gain audience acceptance in any situation—even under stress and regardless of the personalities involved.

Our seminars carry familiar titles:

Presentations: public speaking, sales presentations, videotaped appearances, government testimony, management presentations, serving as "talent" on radio or television commercials (or PSAs), editorial board briefings, and financial presentations (especially meetings of shareholders or security analysts).

Writing: speechwriting for professionals, speechwriting for non-professionals, and feature articles writing.

Interviews: talk shows, crisis response, radio and television interviews, and executive employment interviews.

Each program is custom-designed from a list of approximately 200 instructional units which you select, according to the priorities you assign. The issues and content you specify are used throughout. Thus, each program fulfills your expectations. Participants learn new information rapidly, retain it well, and recall it when they need it most.

For a free list of Rapport seminars available to the public in your area, drop us a note. I would be pleased to show you how our services can provide better skills for you or members of your organization.

Stephen C. Rafe, APR, *President*
Rapport Communications
Dept. HRB P.O. Box 3119
Warrenton, VA 22186
(703) 349-1039